NEW DIRECTIONS FOR TEACHING AND LEARNING

Robert J. Menges, *Northwestern University*
EDITOR-IN-CHIEF

Marilla D. Svinicki, *University of Texas, Austin*
ASSOCIATE EDITOR

Teaching for Diversity

Laura L. B. Border
University of Colorado, Boulder

Nancy Van Note Chism
The Ohio State University, Columbus

EDITORS

Number 49, Spring 1992

JOSSEY-BASS PUBLISHERS
San Francisco

Lee Bell

TEACHING FOR DIVERSITY
Laura L. B. Border, Nancy Van Note Chism (eds.)
New Directions for Teaching and Learning, no. 49
Robert J. Menges, Editor-in-Chief

Microfilm copies of issues and articles are available in 16mm and 35mm, as well as microfiche in 105mm, through University Microfilms Inc., 300 North Zeeb Road, Ann Arbor, Michigan 48106.

LC 85-644763   ISSN 0271-0633   ISBN 1-55542-763-4

NEW DIRECTIONS FOR TEACHING AND LEARNING is part of The Jossey-Bass Higher and Adult Education Series and is published quarterly by Jossey-Bass Publishers, 350 Sansome Street, San Francisco, California 94104. Second-class postage paid at San Francisco, California, and at additional mailing offices. POSTMASTER: Send address changes to Jossey-Bass Publishers, 350 Sansome Street, San Francisco, California 94104.

SUBSCRIPTIONS for 1992 cost $45.00 for individuals and $60.00 for institutions, agencies, and libraries.

EDITORIAL CORRESPONDENCE should be sent to Robert J. Menges, Northwestern University, Center for the Teaching Professions, 2003 Sheridan Road, Evanston, Illinois 60208-2610.

Cover photograph by Richard Blair/Color & Light © 1990.

Printed on acid-free paper in the United States of America.

CONTENTS

EDITORS' NOTES

True dilemmas crop up for colleges and universities grappling with diversity issues. The extent to which diversity questions are rooted in our taken-for-granted assumptions and institutional practices, coupled with the charged atmosphere in which we must act, make the identification, discussion, and resolution of these dilemmas all the more difficult. Yet, corrective action is imperative for a variety of reasons:

The Moral Argument. Higher education professes a belief in the equality of human beings. As we become increasingly aware of the ways in which, consciously or unconsciously, various groups have been oppressed and denied equal participation in higher education, we know that redress and change are necessary.

The Demographic Argument. Projections continue to indicate that the traditional-aged, white, middle- and upper-class college population is shrinking and being replaced by a student pool that is more diverse across virtually every demographic category. Institutions know that they must either accept these new students or downsize dramatically. Self-interest and survival alone dictate that colleges and universities recruit and retain students of both genders who represent a wide variety of racial, ethnic, age, ability, and sexual preference groups.

The Civic Argument. Founded on democratic ideals, the United States professes a belief in an educated citizenry. Our economic structure calls for a skilled work force. There is increased pressure on higher education to continue to produce capable citizens for the future across diverse population categories.

The Enrichment Argument. Central to the notion of "university" is the belief that scholarship is enhanced by the dialogue of multiple viewpoints, that intellectual endeavors can easily stagnate when narrowness of vision or parochial thinking occurs. The new students hold the promise of renewal; connected with the struggle involved in change is the promise of new energy and new ways of thinking.

The Political Argument. Administrators faced with a rise in highly publicized incidents of racism and intolerance, increasingly articulate student interest groups, and popular, legislative, and judicial pressure must view inaction as an untenable course.

Although the reasons for taking action are compelling, the kind and extent of the action needed are the foci of intense dialogue and debate. Arguments about the canon and curriculum, about academic freedom and responsibility, about the articulation between higher education and other societal institutions call for the examination of fundamental issues that have already polarized academics.

1

This volume, *Teaching for Diversity,* is intended to inform the discussion of diversity issues. It speaks to administrators, instructors, faculty/TA developers, and support staff who work in instructional improvement—individuals who must take some action, even in the face of incomplete information and complicated arguments and counterarguments. As such, it emphasizes the practical.

The volume is necessarily limited in scope. First, it focuses solely on teaching and teaching improvement, even though residential life, financial aid, and a host of other factors are involved in diversity efforts. Second, the chapters speak more to the issues of gender, race, and ethnicity than they do to the issues of the ageism, ableism, or sexual preference. Third, they focus much more explicitly on the instructor's role in classroom teaching and learning than on curriculum development or institutional policies and practices.

Terminology is part of the diversity debate, attesting the fundamental ways in which these issues are embedded in our thinking and actions. In this volume, we have tried to avoid terms that currently seem inaccurate and pejorative and to be aware of the ongoing debate over the problems involved in using present U.S. Census classifications to refer to racial and ethnic groups. The essays reflect the unsettled nature of language preference on these issues, the authors have used terminology that is consistent with their experience.

The chapters are arranged in complementary groups. The first three chapters center on the task of opening up the traditional classroom culture to different voices and cultural styles. In Chapter One, Maurianne Adams focuses on the traditional culture of the classroom and the culture of all women and nonwhite male students. In Chapter Two, James A. Anderson and Maurianne Adams examine cognitive styles and their implications for instructional design. And, in Chapter Three, Jonathan Collett and Basilio Serrano focus on genuine inclusiveness.

Intertwined in the classroom culture are communication issues, which are the foci of the next two chapters. Myra Sadker and David Sadker, in Chapter Four, discuss the effects of teacher behavior on student participation in classroom discussion. Frances Maher and Mary Kay Thompson Tetreault, in Chapter Five, describe the struggle to unveil and shift different patterns of communication and power in the feminist classroom.

Implications for developing and implementing programs for instructors are treated in the final three chapters. In Chapter Six, Betty Schmitz, S. Pamela Paul, and James D. Greenberg draw on their experiences at the University of Maryland to describe steps in the planning process. In Chapter Seven, portraits of successful programs are provided by Diane R. vom Saal, Debrah J. Jefferson, and Minion KC Morrison. In Chapter Eight, Laura L. B. Border and Nancy Van Note Chism summarize and provide resources for further study and action.

    We thank our associate editor, Marva Lewis, a graduate student in psychology at the University of Colorado at Boulder, who read the manuscript for accuracy, relevancy, and appropriateness; Noha El-Mahdy, a graduate student in economics at the University of Colorado at Boulder, who assisted with the survey of faculty development programs; Karen Parrish Baker, a graduate research associate at the Center for Teaching Excellence of Ohio State University, who assisted with the data base for the final bibliography; and Selka Lee, Helen Lee, and Julie Wetterholt, students at the University of Colorado at Boulder, who assisted with the preparation of the final manuscript.

> Nancy Van Note Chism
> Laura L. B. Border
> Editors

NANCY VAN NOTE CHISM *is program director for faculty and TA development at the Center for Teaching Excellence, The Ohio State University, Columbus.*

LAURA L. B. BORDER *is director of the Graduate Teacher Program, Graduate School, University of Colorado, Boulder.*

The traditional college classroom has a distinct culture that often constrains the success of students from other cultural backgrounds.

Cultural Inclusion in the American College Classroom

Maurianne Adams

In academe as in any culture, many of the most sacrosanct practices remain unstated, unexamined, and unacknowledged unless or until they are challenged by divergent beliefs from outside the predominant culture. While most faculty and students who have been socialized into the traditional classroom culture are scarcely aware of its existence, those students who have not already been socialized into this culture by previous schooling or a congruent home or community culture often become painfully aware of it. They find that their values and beliefs are in conflict with many traditionally sanctioned classroom procedures that constitute an implicit or hidden curriculum, the *how* of teaching as distinct from the *what*. For example, classroom engagement in competitive or assertive behavior, "talking up" in class, and acceptance of grading curves by which one's gain is another's loss are likely to be in conflict with cultures that do not endorse individual success at the expense of one's peers or that value modesty over assertiveness and cross-age tutoring over competitive interpeer debate.

Furthermore, recent advocates of multicultural classroom practice (Green, 1989) note that traditional instructional models have not even served traditional students all that well. Despite the belief (held by many faculty) that their own college classrooms are culturally neutral and that cultural neutrality is itself an academic norm, the assumptions and values that characterize higher education mainly derive from aspects of European culture shared by nineteenth- and twentieth-century European immigrants to this country, who benefited from higher education to the degree that they already shared a common history and could thereby understand the norms and participate in the behaviors of its educational systems. Yet, this academic culture is narrow in that it rules out nonverbal, empathic, visual, symbolic, or nuanced communication; it neglects the social processes by which interpersonal communication, influence, consensus, and commitment are included in problem solving; it overlooks the social environment as a source of information, together with observation and questioning as information-gathering methodologies; it ignores the values and emotions that nonacademics attach to reasons and facts. And this traditional academic culture is also exclusive in that it privileges those whose families, home communities, and prior schooling are congruent and who accordingly understand, whether or not they accept, the implicit values and behaviors. But to those not socialized, acculturated, or familiar with the ways of higher education, traditional classroom practices seem impersonal, competitive, and off-putting.

Thus, the teaching-learning discourse in college classrooms is in itself a cultural manifestation, presently facing multicultural challenges mounted by students coming to college from non-European racial and ethnic or non-English-speaking backgrounds, by women's questioning of the dominant cultural style, by older adults returning to formal schooling from family or occupational experiences. Examples of this dominant academic cultural style, characterized by the acquisition of course content or disciplinary knowledge and practice, exposition and coverage of information, and the lecture as the expository method of choice, reinforce one set of culture-specific classroom practices—such as linear course sequences, departmentalized academic disciplines, classroom architecture (fixed chairs in straight rows facing lecture podium and chalkboard), and topic-specific textbook chapters—while making alternatives seem awkward or cumbersome, if not altogether unimaginable (Condon, 1986; Kuh and Whitt, 1988; Smith, 1989).

At least two factors can account for why this traditional culture has remained unnoticed. First, although the match of the traditional classroom culture to the learning style of traditional students was never perfect, mismatch was never identified as a frequent cause of student dropout, stop out, shifts of academic majors, or transmutations of learning style accomplished in all sorts of personal and idiosyncratic ways. Ironically, the issue of classroom culture did not emerge for general discussion until it was dramatically raised by divergent cultural values and beliefs and by a level of unsuccessful academic performance at odds with commitments to educational access and opportunity.

But a second factor is presented by the general absence of conscious cultural identity among many Euro-American students. This absence of conscious cultural identity obscures the larger issue of cultural difference, reduces all cultural experience to a single dominant norm, and dismisses as frivolous the culture-consciousness of nontraditional students who want to stress and value their own ethnic roots.

In other words, it has remained possible for students from the dominant culture to disregard the fact that theirs is also a culture and to regard "difference" in culture as meaning merely a greater or lesser departure from their norm. Thus, students from the dominant culture fail to realize that their European-derived belief that higher education provides a bridge to economic and political advancement is based on the assumption that students crossing that bridge start out from a culture that is congruent with traditional college teaching practices. Even the mistakenly termed "model minority" of Asian-American college students can be faced with cruel and unnecessary bicultural dilemmas as they attempt to balance learned cultural values of conformity, modesty, nonassertiveness, interdependence, and cooperation with behavioral expectations of assertion, independence, and individualism demonstrated daily in college classrooms. How confusing it must be, then, for students whose historical and cultural experience has not reflected the belief of the dominant culture that school will equitably provide a vehicle for economic and political advancement, or whose history has involved thwarted efforts toward desegregation, equal educational treatment, or bilingual educational reform. Students from social groups not holding to the dominant cultural framework can too easily be misunderstood by their teachers as underprepared, unmotivated, culturally deprived, or unintelligent.

The role of college faculty in consciously or unconsciously transmitting a dominant cultural system is especially important in addressing present challenges since, in higher education, all roads lead back to the faculty who have control in matters of teaching, evaluation, and curriculum. However, if all roads lead back to the faculty, then the call for multiculturalism—like other fundamental changes in higher education—depends on faculty acceptance and implementation. But the difficulty for faculty of knowing how best to facilitate content-driven learning within a multicultural classroom can lead them, unwittingly, into the stance of seeming to preserve academic standards when in fact transmitting an unexamined culture. It seems urgent, given our new emphasis on multiculturalism, that college faculty become aware of the ways in which the traditional classroom culture excludes or constrains learning for some students and learn how to create environments that acknowledge the cultural diversity that new students bring.

So powerful and pervasive are the folkways of academe as reinforcers of traditional academic practice that it is understandably difficult for college faculty to see beyond their own acculturation and to imagine alternative possibilities for the classroom. The process of designing instructional alternatives engages a faculty member's willingness to consider the many factors that contribute to a college student's immediate learning environment (Joyce and Weil, 1986; West, Farmer, and Wolff, 1991). Rather than simply choosing between one teaching strategy and another, instructional design involves consideration of the learning process from the viewpoint of the learner and intentional selection of strategies with the perspective of the learner and the intentions of the teacher equally in view. The learning process thus involves implicit cultural values that define the social interrelations and behaviors among and between the instructor, classroom peers, and the individual.

The literature on women's socialization and on the educational implications of African-American, Hispanic-American, Asian-American, and Native American cultures suggests not the dismantlement of traditional teaching practices but rather the incorporation of alternative teaching modes that match and engage a broad range of diverse, culturally derived orientations to learning. In this chapter, I review recommendations for change from the multicultural research literature—first from the perspective of gender and second from the perspective of students from African-American, Hispanic-American, Asian-American, and Native American backgrounds—and then outline general principles for creating multicultural classrooms.

The Big Chill: Women in College Classrooms

Recent feminist critiques of traditional academic practice have generated new perspectives and new knowledge. In examining the classroom climate for women, they have portrayed a "chilly" experience of demeaning and discouraging snubs and hostilities toward women too long unrecognized and unacknowledged in traditional, monocultural classrooms (Sandler and Hall, 1986). Whereas the women's movement on college campuses has resulted in the revision of curricular perspectives and course content and the emergence of feminist pedagogy, the present challenge to chilly practices in traditional college classrooms, based on new research on gender socialization and women's development, puts to rest the notion of the college student as a neutral, objective, non-gender-specified "he," whose characteristics accord with academic values of objectivity, autonomy, assertiveness, and individuality (Kuk, 1990; Rodgers, 1990). Current research describes female subjects as oriented more toward affiliation than separation, and preferring collaborative or cooperative interactions over competitive achievements (Gilligan, 1982; Lyons, 1983).

It must be noted that among women, there is variability in experience and in orientation to learning. The dangers of stereotyping based on new findings are as great as ever. Also, the extent to which particular learning styles are chosen rather than innately determined is an issue. For example, the orientation among many women toward collaborative rather than competitive learning environments may reflect socialization within the dominant culture, but it may also reflect a consciously chosen feminist identity with intentional value-oriented behaviors.

Efforts to redress the imbalance in teaching and learning practices of the college classroom include the recommendation of a new emphasis on interpersonal classroom relationships and personally affirming learning environments, matched to the empirical findings on women's development and intellectual orientation and especially the educational concerns of women of color and of all older, returning women whose college educations were interrupted for work, family, or other reasons—women, in other words, who present multiple challenges to traditional academic practices (Pearson, Shavlik, Touchton, 1989; Culley and Portuges, 1985). The resulting controversy about the gender specificity of existing developmental models—and the creation of alternative, possibly complementary developmental models—has generated important research into all areas of women's development and challenged the gender neutrality of existing cognitive developmental models.

The model of cognitive development most widely used among college teachers as a theoretical framework for college instructional design—William Perry's interview-based model of cognitive development—traces the evolution of college students' dualistic right-wrong, either-or certitudes through the uncertainties experienced once multiple options and viewpoints are discovered and the subsequent transformation and relativization of thought with the ultimate discovery of contextually based thinking (Perry, 1968, 1981; Widick and Simpson, 1978). But Perry's model was developed with data collected primarily from white, upper- or middle-class American-born men, so the issue of gender suggested the need to replicate and modify Perry's model or efforts using female subjects exclusively (Clinchy and Zimmerman, 1982) or female subjects in tandem with male subjects (Kitchener and King, 1990; Baxter Magolda, 1990). Women's ways of knowing, initially explored by Belenky, Clinchy, Goldberger, and Tarule (1986, p. 9) to see "what else women might have to say about development" and "alternative routes that were sketchy or missing in Perry's version," emerged as a series of increasingly complex perspectives, starting from silence and reliance on received knowledge and developing toward discovery of subjective knowledge and into procedural connected or separate knowing and constructed knowing.

Based on examination of how women respond to questions about the role of the self as learner and the roles of the instructor and of peers, and of how they grapple with ill-structured real-world dilemmas and questions that cannot be answered with absolute correctness or certainty—occasions where the data are not neat—the new consensus on the existence of different developmental pathways for women depicts women's thought as flexible and variable and men's as more linear and sequential; women tend to collect and appreciate each other's ideas, whereas men tend to debate and evaluate each other's opinions. Accordingly, learning strategies that facilitate the emergence of subjective knowing or the connected dimension of procedural knowing are seen to include the sharing of personal interpretations, classroom use of dialogue and small group discussion rather than debate, experience-based learning, use of journals for registering and tracking new insights and for generating class discussions out of the reports of smaller groups working collaboratively, naturalistic rather than positivist modes of inquiry, and knowledge embedded in social contexts. Modified learning strategies already used in feminist practice (Culley and Portuges, 1985; Bunch and Pollack, 1983) have been endorsed and extended by the new developmental literature on women's ways of learning, as well as the findings related to the chilly classroom for women of color, women with learning or physical disabilities, and older women and to the increasing number of women whose race, ethnicity, social class, religion, sexual orientation, age, multiple responsibilities, and experience present a collective challenge to the prevailing academic culture and educational practice.

Pragmatic efforts to provide more effective learning contexts for women call for the transformation of the role of instructor, especially in the classroom modeling of authority. Research has documented the effectiveness of shared classroom leadership, active involvement to generate multiple student perspectives, challenges to women to establish and defend their own viewpoints, reinforcement of independent thinking, creative uses of peer learning groups, carefully designed collaborative efforts with clearly established goals, structured group projects, new methods for opening up discussion or observing discussions, and a new vocabulary of value terms (nurturing, empowerment, collaboration) representing a new culture for learning. Although female and male orientations are seen only as "predispositions that inhere in the structure of the human life cycle" (Gilligan, 1988, pp. 4-5), educational practices that favor one orientation may not equally serve the other. Classroom debates focused on concepts of justice may support the male orientation, while the debate format models a win-lose mindset. An alternative approach, more favorable to an orientation toward connection and caring, might be based on dialogue discussions in which students draw on each other's expertise, using the teacher for focus and support, or on collaborative projects that strengthen relationships among students. Although the association between these two orientations and gender is such that men and women each on occasion use both, the tendency for women to favor connection and care, and for men to favor separation or justice, remains strong (Gilligan and Attanucci, 1988; Lyons, 1983).

The acceptance of women's ways of knowing as a difference to be responded to, not a deficit to be remedied, parallels in important dimensions the acceptance of ways of knowing for students from cultural backgrounds whose values and beliefs depart from those of the traditional academic culture. It may well be that Belenky and her associates' findings of two orientations, one separate and one connected, within procedural knowing (itself a form of knowing congruent with established college practices) demonstrate the biculturation of many Euro-American college women who have managed to adapt their learning orientation to that of the traditional college classroom, while maintaining a second subjective or connected orientation to themselves. The research on African-American, Hispanic-American, Asian-American, and Native American women incorporates many of the general recommendations already noted above, while emphatically rejecting the notion that these students do or should acculturate in order to survive academically. The model of a multicultural classroom that enhances bicultural learning flows directly from the research on learning styles resulting from the intersection of gender and racial or ethnic culture.

From Cultural Deficit to Cultural Difference

The cultural pathways that differentiate African-American, Hispanic-American, Asian-American, and Native American cultures' ways of knowing from ways of knowing traditionally sanctioned by college instruction and assessment have been described in a school ethnography research tradition that documents the ways in which students from nondominant ethnic groups experience incompatibility with the dominant culture of higher education (Shade, 1989; Tharp, 1989). This research calls attention to the ways in which distinctive racial and ethnic cultures experienced in families and home communities interact with historical and personal experiences of discrimination and racism. Thus, there are reasons, beyond the socialization patterns noted in the case of women, why the cultural styles of students from non-European, nonwhite racial and ethnic backgrounds—often the first generation of family members to attend college—are not likely to match the dominant culture of higher education. The situation for African-American, Hispanic-American, Asian-American, and Native American college students, already complicated as we saw in the case of women by the deficit burden of cultural difference, is further complicated, unlike the case of Euro American women, by several additional considerations.

First, there is no consensus within the research tradition to directly connect cultural ways of knowing based on race or ethnicity to classroom learning, although some studies of cognitive style present related implications. While educators agree that students learn in different ways and that teachers should take account of such differences in their instructional strategies, "no consensus exists as to which differences matter in terms of learning. There is, in fact, active disagreement as to whether the cultural backgrounds of students should be singled out for attention" (Green, 1989, p. 141).

Second, and closely related to the question of whether or not cultural backgrounds should be singled out, there is the danger of creating new stereotypes. Broad generalizations about culturally different learning styles can too easily be misunderstood as euphemisms for deficits calling for remediation or acculturation of the student rather than flexibility and responsiveness from the college instructor. The identification of cultural styles with broadly defined racial or linguistic minorities—African, Asian, and Hispanic Americans, for example—blurs finer distinctions among ethnic cultures that students from Cape Verdean or Jamaican, Vietnamese or mainland Chinese, and Cuban or Puerto Rican backgrounds, for example, bring to their college tasks. It blurs the complexities for students from biracial families or from multiracial neighborhoods. It ignores the situation of students from monocultural communities and prior schooling for whom the experience of a predominantly white college campus may constitute a first, direct, conscious awareness of minority status. There are generational effects (whether in North America or in college) and there are multiple sources of oppression as race and ethnicity intersect with gender, social class, economic status, physical or learning disabilities, age, religion, and sexual orientation. Generalizations from the research on cultural learning styles have to be seasoned by the multiple cultural crosscurrents that students are likely to have experienced.

Third, and in addition to the risk of stereotyping college students on the basis of racial, linguistic, or cultural characteristics, there is the interaction of cultural styles with purposeful survival techniques within oppressive social conditions. For example, for African-American students, commitment to strong family responsibilities or community ties may express a value within their respective cultures or reflect a transformation of community survival strategies into a more conscious Afrocentric identity (Jones, 1990).

Whatever the source or purpose, cultural style reflects beliefs, values, and norms that support styles or orientations toward the goal of learning. College faculty would be deeply mistaken to confuse the stylistic differences among students with their intrinsic capabilities. Learning style—like teaching style—reflects a means toward an end and involves pedagogies and procedures that are easily confused with the actual learning goals themselves.

The research on cultural style reinforces the recommendations in the literature on women's ways of knowing for an instructional balance between connected and collaborative learning and traditional classroom norms. The increasing body of findings on cultural differences has led researchers to develop new frameworks for analyzing the classroom with respect to multiculturalism. One such framework is the taxonomy of psychocultural variables for educational practice proposed by Tharp (1989) for teachers attempting to distinguish various aspects of cultural differences. Briefly, these variables include *elements of social organization,* such as whole class or small group activities and collaborative or assisted demonstrations or performances as distinct from expository methods; *sociolinguistics,* such as patterns of question and discussion, length of wait time between answers and follow-up questions, and culturally sanctioned participation patterns; *cognitive style,* which includes orientation toward the visual or verbal, holistic or analytic presentations, use of context, and sequential patterns of thought; and *motivation,* which refers to cultural differences between achievement and affiliation motives, and family and peer group solidarity as a cultural framework for attainment and recognition.

Another area of research on cultural style, especially relevant for college faculty, concerns predictors of academic success in college for African-American students. These predictors include culturally relevant indexes such as leadership within a cultural-racial peer context, availability of a strong support person, community service, nontraditional knowledge, understanding of racism, and positive self-concept (Sedlacek, 1987). Not only are these indexes related to cultural difference as opposed to deficit, they are also tied to nontraditional students' capacity to deal with overt discrimination (understanding of racism) and to rid themselves of internalized negative stereotypes (positive self-concept). It is important for college teachers to become aware of the stages of social identity development by which nontraditional students gradually transform their internalized aspects of negative stereotyping, learned from an oppressive social context with reference to race, gender, religion, or sexual orientation, into positive self-concepts. These stages of social identity development have significant behavioral and motivational indicators and characteristics that are described in social identity development models, many of which are directly related to the selection of teaching strategies (Cross, 1991; Jones, 1990; Wright, 1987; Jackson, 1976). Despite differences among students, it is also important to consider white and nonwhite social and cultural interactions in college classrooms that suggest shared bicultural values distinct from values reported by each cultural group separately. This bicultural agreement suggests an instructional model that recognizes elements of different cultural orientations but also incorporates common cultural elements (Kochman, 1981; Carter, 1990).

General Principles for Creating the Multicultural Classroom

From these findings on cultural styles, one can begin to establish as a general principle that a college teacher's explicit and ongoing attention to the cultural assumptions behind many aspects of classroom teaching will facilitate the learning process for students from all cultural traditions, it will also dramatize the instructor's recognition that not all social groups share the same history of relatively positive, prior educational experience. This principle clarifies for members of the dominant culture that knowledge is itself a social product and that the hegemonic Western educational traditions do not constitute a legitimate measure of educational success. A college teacher's modeling of cultural variation and reciprocity illustrates a stance and attitude by which members of dominant (majority) and subordinate (minority) cultures become aware of each other's cultural differences and become more sensitive transcultural communicators.

For the pragmatic purpose of creating a classroom environment that respects diversity, several principles germane to women's development hold as well for students from African-American, Hispanic-American, Asian-American, and Native American backgrounds: In recognizing (1) cultural differences, not deficits, among students (2) we must create learning environments for all, not some, students, (3) based on multicultural, not ethnocentric, principles of teaching and learning that are inclusive rather than exclusive, responsive and flexible rather than fixed or predetermined, and derived from (4) cross-cultural or multicultural models of cultural reciprocity and interaction that ultimately benefit all students.

It is obvious that multiculturally responsive teaching calls for a substantial commitment by college teachers, for whom such an agenda may well appear daunting, time consuming, emotionally demanding, full of pitfalls and unpleasant surprises, potentially unrewarded by senior colleagues, difficult to imagine in lecture sections of several hundred students, and possibly inefficient in its use of the fifty-minute class session already crowded by discipline-based syllabus coverage. Considering also the semblance of conflict in the gender and ethnic cultural implications for instructional design, it is not surprising that many college faculty continue to feel more comfortable emphasizing the *what* of curriculum reform over the *how* of instructional practice. Clearly, any review of one's own cultural assumptions, along with those that support current practice, involves a long-term commitment, not a short-term project. Moreover, a long-term view also must take into account that the social factors shaping one's students are themselves in flux and reflect processes of change in intergroup relations.

Nonetheless, despite changes due to forces such as demographics, movements toward social justice, and efforts to develop multicultural literacy among children as well as adults, some familiar teaching practices remain that provide stable reference points for college teaching. At the least we can draw one general conclusion from the extensive literature on gender and ethnic cultural styles referred to earlier, and that is the importance of developing a repertoire of flexible and variable teaching strategies. These strategies can usefully be described as points along several of the continua described earlier: from active to passive student participation, concrete to abstract modes of thought, visual or auditory to verbal modes of representation, and experimental and dramatic to reflective and observational expository methodologies (for specific teaching strategies derived from these observations, see Anderson and Adams, this volume). In reviewing one's own teaching methods in light of learning orientations suggested by women's ways of knowing, for example, a college teacher may decide to balance subjective exploration of course content with objective presentations, or to invite his or her students to personalize the subject matter with examples from their experience, or to utilize collaborative learning projects instead of loose-ended classroom discussion. Teachers might try what

Belenky, Clinchy, Goldberger, and Tarule (1986) call "connected teaching" or "sharing the process" to try on the facilitating role of "midwife teachers," as opposed to the direct-deposit method of "banker teachers."

These and other adjustments to traditional college practice suggested by the women's way of knowing literature parallel recommendations from the racial and ethnic cultural style literature. There also we see the importance of drawing on social relationships rather than exclusively valuing the separate and objective, of balancing holistic or contextual presentations with separate and analytic explanations, of acknowledging that learning can just as well be viewed from personal, self, and social orientations as from the objective and impersonal, of considering the role of feelings of and responses from other people, and of developing visual and mimetic as well as verbal proficiencies.

Earlier it was noted that all roads to multicultural classrooms lead back to the college teacher. More exactly, all roads lead back to the flexibility of a college instructor's teaching repertoire, and his or her readiness to draw on a range of teaching styles for a variety of ends: First, a variable, flexible repertoire of teaching strategies enables college teachers to match the cultural styles of students from targeted social groups in their college classes. Second, because such teaching is effective teaching, it can match individual learning differences among traditional students as well. Third, a college teacher's repertoire of flexible and variable teaching strategies exemplifies for all of his or her students the multicultural value of reciprocity rather than the monocultural expectation of acculturation. That is, a mixed repertoire enables all students in a college classroom to experience an environment that equalizes cultural styles rather than requires minority cultural styles to give way and acculturate or adapt to the dominant mode, maintaining thereby the cultural edge of students from the dominant culture. An environment of cultural equality teaches from strength to strength and facilitates the development of several cultural styles and skills not in the repertoire of any one learner, regardless of his or her cultural background. Finally, active engagement in collaborative group learning enterprises fosters student-to-student and student-to-teacher experiences across cultural differences, establishing a better basis for mutual understanding and trust.

References

Baxter Magolda, M. B. "Gender Differences in Epistemological Development." *Journal of College Student Development,* 1990, *31* (4), 555–561.

Belenky, M. F., Clinchy, B. M., Goldberger, N. R., and Tarule, J. M. *Women's Ways of Knowing: The Development of Self, Body, and Mind.* New York: Basic Books, 1986.

Bunch, C., and Pollack, S. *Learning Our Way: Essays in Feminist Education.* Trumansburg, N.Y.: Crossing Press, 1983.

Carter, R. T. "Cultural Value Differences Between African Americans and White Americans." *Journal of College Student Development,* 1990, *31* (1), 71–79.

Clinchy, B. M., and Zimmerman, C. "Epistemology and Agency in the Development of Under-graduate Woman." In P. Perun (ed.), *The Undergraduate Woman: Issues in Educational Equity.* Lexington, Mass.: Heath, 1982.

Condon, J. C. "The Ethnographic Classroom." In J. M. Civikly (ed.), *Communicating in College Classrooms.* New Directions in Teaching and Learning, no. 26. San Francisco: Jossey-Bass, 1986.

Cross, W. E., Jr. *Shades of Black: Diversity in African-American Identity.* Philadelphia: Temple University Press, 1991.

Culley, M., and Portuges, C. *Gendered Subjects: The Dynamics of Feminist Teaching.* Boston: Routledge & Kegan Paul, 1985.

Gilligan, C. *In a Different Voice: Psychological Theory and Women's Development.* Cambridge, Mass.: Harvard University Press, 1982.

Gilligan, C. "Remapping the Moral Domain: New Images of Self and Relationship." In C. Gilligan, J. V. Ward, and J. H. Taylor (eds.), *Mapping the Moral Domain.* Center for the Study of Gender, Education, and Human Development, no. 2. Cambridge, Mass.: Harvard University Press, 1988.

Gilligan, C., and Attanucci, B. "Two Moral Orientations." In C. Gilligan, J. V. Ward, and J. H. Taylor (eds.), *Mapping the Moral Domain: A Contribution of Women's Thinking to Psychological Theory and Education.* Center for the Study of Gender, Education, and Human Development. Cambridge, Mass.: Harvard University Press, 1988.

Green, M. F. (ed.). *Minorities on Campus: A Handbook for Enhancing Diversity.* Washington, D.C.: American Council on Education, 1989.

Jackson, B. W. "Black Identity Development." In L. Golubschick and B. Persky (eds.), *Urban Social and Educational Issues.* Dubuque, Iowa: Kendall/Hunt, 1976.

Jones, W. T. "Perspectives on Ethnicity." In L. V. Moore (ed.), *Evolving Theoretical Perspectives on Students.* New Directions for Student Services, no. 51. San Francisco: Jossey-Bass, 1990.

Joyce, B., and Weil, M. *Models of Teaching.* (3rd ed.) Englewood Cliffs, N.J.: Prentice Hall, 1986.

Kitchener, K. S., and King, P. M. "The Reflective Judgment Model: Ten Years of Research." In M. I. Commons, C. Armon, L. Kohlberg, F. A. Richards, T. A. Grotzer, and J. D. Sinnott (eds.), *Adult Development.* Vol. 3: *Models and Methods in the Study of Adolescent and Adult Thought.* New York: Praeger, 1990.

Kochman, T. *Black and White Styles in Conflict.* Chicago: University of Chicago Press, 1981.

Kuh, G. D., and Whitt, E. J. *The Invisible Tapestry: Culture in American Colleges and Universities.* ASHE-ERIC Higher Education Reports, no. 1. Washington, D.C.: Association for the Study of Higher Education, 1988.

Kuk, L. "Perspectives on Gender Differences." In L. V. Moore (ed.), *Evolving Theoretical Perspectives on Students.* New Directions for Student Services, no. 51. San Francisco: Jossey-Bass, 1990.

Lyons, N. "Two Perspectives: On Self, Relationships, and Morality." *Harvard Educational Review,* 1983, 53 (2), 125–145.

Pearson, C. S., Shavlick, D. L., and Touchton, J. G. (eds.). *Educating the Majority: Women Challenge Tradition in Higher Education.* New York: American Council on Education/Macmillan, 1989.

Perry, W. G. *Forms of Intellectual and Moral Development in the College Years.* New York: Holt, Rinehart & Winston, 1968.

Perry, W. G. "Cognitive and Ethical Growth: The Making of Meaning." In A. W. Chickering and Associates (eds.), *The Modern American College: Fostering Higher Learning Through Curriculum and Student Transfer.* San Francisco: Jossey-Bass, 1981.

Rodgers, R. F. "Recent Theories and Research Underlying Student Development." In D. G. Creamer and Associates (eds.), *College Student Development Theory and Practice for the 1990s.* Alexandria, Va.: American College Personnel Association, 1990.

Sandler, B. R., and Hall, R. M. *The Campus Climate Revisited: Chilly for Women Faculty, Administrators, and Graduate Students.* Washington, D.C.: Project on the Status and Education of Women, Association of American Colleges, 1986.

Sedlacek, W. E. "Black Students on White Campuses: 20 Years of Research." *Journal of College Student Personnel,* 1987, *28* (6), 484–496.

Shade, B.J.R. (ed.). *Culture, Style, and the Educative Process.* Springfield, Ill.: Thomas, 1989.

Smith, D. G. *The Challenge of Diversity: Involvement or Alienation in the Academy?* ASHE-ERIC Higher Education Reports, no. 5. Washington, D.C.: Association for the Study of Higher Education, 1989.

Tharp, R. G. "Psychocultural Variables and Constants: Effects on Teaching and Learning in Schools." *American Psychologist,* 1989, *44* (2), 349–359.

West, C. K., Farmer, J. A., and Wolff, P. M. *Instructional Design: Implications from Cognitive Science.* Englewood Cliffs, N.J.: Prentice Hall, 1991.

Widick, C., and Simpson, D. "Developmental Concepts in College Instruction." In C. A. Parker (ed.), *Encouraging Development in College Students.* Minneapolis: University of Minnesota Press, 1978.

Wright, D. J. "Minority Students: Developmental Beginnings." In D. J. Wright (ed.), *Responding to the Needs of Today's Minority Students.* New Directions for Student Services, no. 38. San Francisco: Jossey-Bass, 1987.

MAURIANNE ADAMS is lecturer in human development, faculty in the Social Justice and Diversity Education Project, and director for Instructional Development and Social Issues Education (Residential Academic Programs) in the School of Education, University of Massachusetts, Amherst.

The practice of taking student learning style into account while designing instruction is important to the success of all students.

Acknowledging the Learning Styles of Diverse Student Populations: Implications for Instructional Design

James A. Anderson, Maurianne Adams

Perhaps at no other time has there been more discussion, thinking, and tension about issues in higher education than there is now. Of major concern is the question of how to value and structure classroom teaching in light of the challenges to established teaching modes brought about by the increasing social and cultural diversity of college students. The increased emphasis on the enhancement of undergraduate education across disciplines has produced a surge of inquiry in our academic institutions. As colleges begin to examine the dominant paradigms and canons in the academic disciplines and their methods of instruction, they are inevitably struck by the motivational and learning characteristics of students who are different from the white, middle-class males who traditionally have been the dominant group in the undergraduate population. Thus, issues concerning teaching effectiveness and excellence are increasingly tied to issues of diversity. As Banks (1991) suggests, diverse groups are often only discussed in terms of their global characteristics, when, in fact, we should be examining the interplay of social and cultural diversity with learning styles, curriculum content, and instructional styles.

One of the most significant challenges that university instructors face is to be tolerant and perceptive enough to recognize learning differences among their students. Many instructors do not realize that students vary in the way that they process and understand information. The notion that all students' cognitive skills are identical at the collegiate level smacks of arrogance and elitism by sanctioning one group's style of learning while discrediting the styles of others. Differences in learning (or learning style) do not imply the deficits often associated with men of color or with women students.

Effective teaching cannot be limited to the delivery of information; rather, it needs to be based on a model of minds at work. Effective teachers are those who involve all of their students in learning how to learn. This generative process of learning is most effective when instructors (1) affirm the presence and validity of diverse learning styles and (2) maximize the climate or conditions for learning in the classroom through the deliberate use of instructional design principles that take account of learning differences and increase the possibilities of success for all students.

Learning Styles and Diversity

The recent emphasis on social and cultural diversity in the college classroom reflects the recognition that groups of students enter college with variations in the following areas: (1) social relational skills, values, and characteristics, (2) information-processing orientations and skills, (3) communication patterns, (4) learning styles and strategies, (5) motivational styles, and (6) psychological characteristics. These differences cannot be isolated simplistically along the lines of race, culture, or gender alone; in fact, myriad factors may influence the evolution of a particular style for a particular student. Much debate and controversy has been generated during the last decade by the idea that stylistic preferences can be used to characterize entire groups of people, especially groups identified along ethnic or cultural lines. Although the research base to date does not demonstrate definitive links between learning style and race, culture, or gender, consistent cultural and educational findings across such disciplines as psychology, sociology, anthropology, and linguistics suggest some correlations. But for college teachers, the central question is not whether students from different social and cultural backgrounds approach knowledge in ways that are unique and functional within their respective indigenous home environments. Rather, the critical issues seem to be the following: (1) Are stylistic differences so pronounced that we can make clear distinctions among groups? (2) Have the sociocultural experiences of diverse populations been so encapsulated that their fundamental ways of knowing about the world are categorically distinct from the ways of the white, male population? (3) Does a focus on differences suggest that certain groups are deficient and need different treatment and access? (4) Is it feasible to discuss changes or adaptions in instructional style in order to accommodate diverse learning styles?

It is often difficult to identify where to begin to answer such questions because of their complexity. There exists a confusing array of definitions of learning style, a term often used interchangeably with cognitive style or learning ability (Claxton and Murrell, 1987; Tharp, 1989). The research literature on learning style differences among traditional student populations reflects the striking nature of these differences in most college classrooms, quite apart from considerations of social and cultural differences (Claxton and Murrell, 1987; Kolb, 1981; Witkin and Moore, 1975). This literature pays some attention to gender differences (Gelwick, 1985) as well as to older adult returnees to college (Cross, 1987; Pearson, Shavlick, and Touchton, 1989). The learning style literature also calls attention to the diversity within nontraditional student populations (Ramirez and Castaneda, 1974; Anderson, 1988) in a growing body of research that demonstrates the cultural component of learning style differences (Shade, 1989; Tharp, 1989). Messick (1976) concluded that ethnic groups, independent of socioeconomic status, display characteristic patterns of abilities that are strikingly different from one another. For example, research in cognitive psychology and anthropology provides ample evidence of differences among Americans from African, Asian, Hispanic, and Native American, as distinct from European, heritages. These differences occur in information processing, memory, problem solving, and thinking. In many cases, the differences appear even when disparate samples are matched for socioeconomic status. Lesser (1976, p. 137) found that "people who share a common cultural background will also share, to a certain extent, common patterns of intellectual abilities, thinking styles, and interests." More specifically, studies that have examined different groups' orientations to cultural values (human nature, nature, human activity, time, social organizations) support the contention that nontraditional groups who share common conceptualizations about basic values, beliefs, and behaviors exhibit similar socialized differences and stylistic learning preferences (Carter, 1990; Kluckhohn and Strodbeck, 1961).

Cooper (1981) has highlighted the impact of stylistic differences in language among African Americans. Ramirez and Price-Williams (1974) have focused on the cognitive styles of Hispanic students. Moore (1988) has examined the learning styles of Native American students. Hale-Benson (1986) and Shade (1989) further document the unique cultural, learning, and motivational styles of various racial and ethnic groups. Generally, the pattern that emerges is that these students demonstrate competence in social interactions and peer cooperation, performance, visual perception, symbolic expression, and narrative and therefore are less comfortable with tasks that require independence, competition, or verbal skills. For example, Native American students appear in many situations to be more skilled in performing tasks than in verbal expression, more visual than auditory linguistic, more oriented toward observation or imitation than toward verbal instruction, and more comfortable with spatial than with sequential activities and with group, peer, or cross-age learning projects than with individual question-and-answer sessions. Chicano socialization endorses cooperative interactions oriented toward helping others rather than individualistic competition. African-American students often communicate through peer relationships that support group learning or group (but not individual) competitions, simulations, and role plays (Kochman, 1981; Hale-Benson, 1986; Shade, 1989; Pearson, Shavlick, and Touchton, 1989; Tharp, 1989).

Some of the culturally distinctive patterns and tendencies that appear to differentiate the learning orientations of non-European and nonwhite students from those of traditional college populations show up in recent research on female college students (Kuk, 1990). In research discussed more fully in Chapter One of this volume, Gilligan (1982) and Baker Miller (1986) found typical and recurrent differences from the white, male norm in their female subjects: affiliation rather than separation, an identity oriented toward relationships rather than toward autonomy, and a preference for collaborative or cooperative interaction rather than competitive achievement. Similarly, Baxter Magolda (1989, 1990) notes stylistic differences between college men and women, especially in their orientation toward self, peers, and instructors.

Teaching Styles and Strategies

Many descriptions of learning style and cognitive style are based on bipolar distributions of characteristics, with each pole having adaptive value for different learning environments (analytical/relational or field sensitivity/independence or impulsive/reflective). These constructs, while admittedly more simplified than the reality that they are designed to describe, have descriptive value with respect to racial, ethnic, and gender differences among college students. For example, Anderson (1988) has looked at the differences between analytical and relational learners. Table 2.1 highlights the characteristics associated with each style. One can note from Table 2.1 that relational learners—unlike analytical learners, who tend to match the traditional teaching mode of higher education—place an emphasis on affective and reality-based learning, a broad and personal approach to the processing of information, a search for relevance and personal meaning in what is taught, and a need for qualitative feedback.

Similarly, Witkin and Moore (1975) employed the bipolar global categories of field dependence and independence to refer to the manner in which learners process and structure information in the environment. According to this scheme, people tend to develop stylistic preferences for certain environmental cues. Persons who utilize a field-dependent or field-sensitive orientation process information from their entire surroundings. In the classroom they are as concerned about the human relational interaction and communication style of the instructor as they are about the delivery of the content; they do not see the two as separate. They also expect the instructor to identify with them in a holistic way as students and as individuals. Conflict, or at least a disconcerting feeling, begins to emerge when students experience teaching styles that do not match their expectations.

It can readily be seen that research on the learning styles of white

Table 2.1. Characteristics of Student Learning Styles

Relational Style	Analytical Style
1. Perceive information as part of total picture	1. Able to disembed information from total picture (focus on detail)
2. Exhibit improvisational and intuitive thinking	2. Exhibit sequential and structured thinking
3. More easily learn materials that have a human, social content and are characterized by experiential/cultural relevance	3. More easily learn materials that are inanimate and impersonal
4. Good memory for verbally presented ideas and information, especially if relevant	4. Good memory for abstract ideas and irrelevant information
5. More task-oriented concerning nonacademic areas	5. More task-oriented concerning academics
6. Influenced by authority figures' expression of confidence or doubt in students' ability	6. Not greatly affected by the opinions of others
7. Prefer to withdraw from unstimulating task performance	7. Show ability to persist at unstimulating tasks
8. Style conflicts with the traditional school environment	8. Style matches most school environments

women and men and of women students of color can be combined with the kinds of global constructs that Anderson, Witkin, Moore, and others have delineated to profile differences in learning. Research drawing on the constructs of field sensitivity and field independence tends to find that white females and African-American, Native American, and Hispanic-American males and females fall toward the relational, field-sensitive end of the continuum, whereas Euro-American and Asian-American males fall toward the analytical, field-independent end of the spectrum. These differences have distinct implications for preferences in student instruction and teaching strategies. One initial approach to teaching change might be to develop a sense of the expectations of students and instructors as they simply interact with one another. Such interactions guide the more formal dimensions of the teaching-learning dyad. Table 2.2 offers one example of the expectations that two different types of students exhibit. Table 2.3 presents a comparison of teaching styles based on the same two types of orientation. It should be clear through comparison of Tables 2.2 and 2.3 that the expectations of field-dependent students will generally not be realized when the learning conditions are structured by field-independent instructors.

Table 2.2. What Students Expect from Instructors, Based on Preferred Style

Field-Dependent Orientation	Field-Independent Orientation
1. To give support, show interest, be emotional	1. To focus on task and objectives
2. To provide guidance, modeling, and constructive feedback	2. To encourage independence and flexibility
3. To provide verbal and nonverbal cues to support words	3. To provide commands and messages directly and articulately
4. To minimize professional distance	4. To maximize professional distance
5. To seek opinions when making decisions and incorporate affective considerations criteria	5. To make decisions based on analysis of problems and objectives
6. To identify with values and needs of students	6. To identify with goals and objectives of task

Table 2.3. Field-Dependent and Field-Independent Teaching Strategies

Field-Dependent	Field-Independent
1. Focuses on needs, feelings, and interests of students	1. Focuses on task
2. Acts as a consultant or supervisor in the classroom	2. Fosters modeling and imitation
3. Uses an informal approach and elicits class discussion	3. Uses a formal, lecture-oriented approach
4. Uses personal rewards	4. Uses impersonal rewards
5. Encourages group achievement	5. Encourages individual achievement
6. Narrates and humanizes concepts	6. Emphasizes facts and principles
7. Identifies with class	7. Remains emotionally detached

Designing Flexible and Responsive Instruction

Clearly, a diverse student population means that there is greater variability in learning styles in the same classroom than typically exists with a homogeneous population of traditional college students. While identification of styles with particular social and cultural groups helps alert instructors to important differences among their students, a full range of instructional strategies should be employed in the classroom in any event. For college teachers in search of specific instructional strategies that match a full range of cultural characteristics, it is especially helpful to use, within a well-established learning style model, a framework that already incorporates elements of gender and racial-ethnic culture (see Adams, this volume). In this sense, a framework for developing a multicultural teaching repertoire can be seen as simply an extension of effective teaching for all students. From this perspective, the experiential learning model of David Kolb, which already challenges traditional classroom practice by providing a flexible framework for instructional design, can now be brought to bear on the cultural style differences referred to in the preceding sections. The model includes, but also goes beyond, some of the bipolar opposites adduced in the cultural style research based on the constructs of field sensitivity and field independence. Kolb's experiential learning model is rooted in a theory of learning that affirms all major aspects of active learning, usefully accounting for an array of individual (or, in our case, culturally derived) differences (Kolb, 1981, 1984; Smith and Kolb, 1986; Svinicki and Dixon, 1987).

Kolb's experiential learning model is derived from a model of social learning that connects variability of individual learning style to flexibility in learning context. As shown in Figure 2.1, the four dimensions of the cycle include, in clockwise cyclical movement, a learner's immersion in concrete experience, followed by the process of observing and reflecting on self or others from a single personal viewpoint or from multiple viewpoints, followed by the logically shaped or inductive systematic conclusions or abstractions, and, finally, the empirical testing of action plans that arise from the abstract concepts and, in turn, give rise to new experiences, thereby starting the learning cycle anew at a greater level of complexity.

Figure 2.1. The Experiential Learning Model

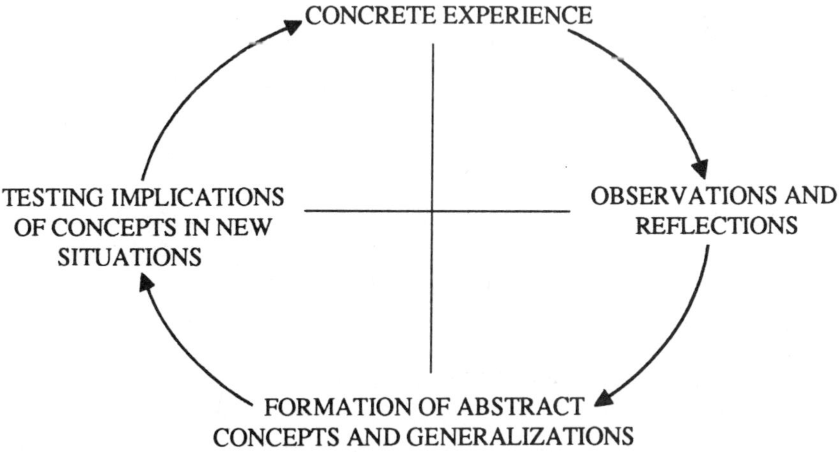

CONCRETE EXPERIENCE

TESTING IMPLICATIONS OF CONCEPTS IN NEW SITUATIONS

OBSERVATIONS AND REFLECTIONS

FORMATION OF ABSTRACT CONCEPTS AND GENERALIZATIONS

Figure 2.1 also represents the cyclical interaction among two inter-secting dimensions of the learning process, which lie at the ends of two intersecting axes. Both intersecting dimensions are bipolar, representing, on the one hand, how we take in or perceive information (the vertical axis, on a continuum from concrete to abstract) and, on the other hand, how we process or transform what we take in (the horizontal axis, on a continuum from reflective observation across to active testing or experimentation). While each of the four aspects is essential to learning when taken by itself, each can also be individually or culturally understood to represent a pre-ferred learning style, often giving rise within college settings to choices of academic majors and career choices (Kolb, 1981, 1984; Smith and Kolb, 1986) as well as to preferences in and mismatches to college teaching practices. Thus, there are significant instructional incentives to include learning strategies from each of the four aspects of the cycle, both to match the preferred style for students of each type who attend our classes and to ensure student exposure to each of the four essential ingredients of an inclusive learning process.

Classroom activities can be designed or selected to match specific aspects of the cycle, and planned sequences of selected activities will not only lead students through the learning cycle on any segment of course material but will also more or less accord with the different learning style orientations of students, although specific activities may perfectly well fit any one of several aspects of the cycle depending on a teacher's presenta-tions, instructions, and interpretations of the activities (Smith and Kolb, 1986; Svinicki and Dixon, 1987). Figures 2.2 and 2.3 represent a number of college learning activities already in the learning style literature that are matched to each aspect of the learning cycle, any one of which can be further adapted for individual or group, independent or collaborative, in-class or out-of-class student activities. Thus, in light of the multicultural instructional concerns of this chapter, a college teacher might substitute as intersecting axes several new bipolar continua derived from the cultural style literature—continua from competitive to collaborative, or from separate to connected, or from global and holistic to analytic, or from visual to verbal.

Figure 2.4, which takes a continuum from active (student as actor) to passive (student as receiver) and moves it around the four aspects of the learning cycle as hands on a clock, suggests a way in which other continua derived from the multicultural style literature might similarly be set in motion. These multicultural continua can be substituted for—or superim-posed on—the vertical or horizontal axes of the learning cycle in order to arrive at a single instructional design tool that incorporates recommenda-tions from the multicultural literature. These substitutions would adjust the concrete/abstract dimension of perceiving or taking in information (the vertical axis) to also include specific relational-analytic or inductive-deduc-tive or visual-verbal alternatives of perceiving and taking in information

Figure 2.2. Learning Strengths and Preferred Learning Situations

	LEARNING STRENGTHS	PREFERRED LEARNING SITUATIONS
Concrete Experience	Learning by *intuition* Learning from specific experiences Relating to people Sensitivity to people Sensitivity to feelings	Learning from new experiences, games, role plays, and so on Peer feedback and discussion Personalized counseling Teacher as coach/helper
Reflective Observation	Learning by *perception* Careful observation before making judgments Viewing things from different perspectives Introversion—looking inward for the meaning	Lectures Opportunities to take an observer role, to see different perspectives on an issue Objective tests of one's knowledge about an issue Teacher as guide/task master
Abstract Conceptualization	Learning by *thinking* Logical analysis of ideas Systematic planning Deductive thinking—acting on the basis of one's understanding of a situation	Theory readings Study time alone Clear, well-structured presentation of ideas Teacher as communicator of information
Active Experimentation	Learning by *doing* Ability to get things done Risk taking Extroversion—acting to influence people and events	Opportunities to practice and receive feedback Small group discussions Projects and individualized, self-paced, learning activities Teacher as role model on how to do it

Note: This is a summary of learning strengths and preferred learning situations that have been discovered by learning style research. It is meant to better equip the teacher/trainer in creating programs and curricula that meet the needs of each student.

Source: Smith and Kolb, 1986, p. 28. Copyright © McBer & Company, 1985. This material may not be reproduced in any way, except with the written permission of McBer & Company, 137 Newbury Street, Boston, MA 02116, (617) 437-7080.

**Figure 2.3. Instructional Activities That Support Different Aspects
of the Learning Cycle**

CONCRETE EXPERIENCE
readings
examples
fieldwork
laboratories
problem sets
trigger films
observations
simulations/games
primary text reading

ACTIVE EXPERIMENTATION   REFLECTIVE OBSERVATION
projects   logs
fieldwork   journals
homework   discussion
laboratory   brainstorming
case study   thought questions
simulations   rhetorical questions

ABSTRACT CONCEPTUALIZATION
lecture
papers
projects
analogies
model building

Source: Svinicki and Dixon, 1987, p. 142. Reprinted with permission of The Helen Dwight Reid Educational Foundation. Published by Heldrefh Publications, 4000 Albermarle Street, NW, Washington, D.C. 20016. Copyright © 1987.

both concretely and abstractly as in Figure 2.5. Similar substitutions would adjust the active/reflective dimension of processing, transforming, and acting on information (the horizontal axis) to include considerations of achievement or affiliation as rewards or motives, competition or collaboration as multiple perspective and action orientations, or culturally sanctioned separate or connected alternatives for making sense of new information as in Figure 2.6. If we vary the degree to which the student's role is active or passive, we can visualize it using the original illustrative model shown in Figure 2.4 and set in clockwise motion the bipolar continua shown in Figures 2.5 and 2.6.

This is only one of various conceptual models and instructional design frameworks available in the learning style literature that either reflects multicultural research or can be adjusted by the college teacher for multicultural use (see Condon, 1986; Smith and Kolb, 1986; Svinicki and Dixon, 1987; Green, 1989; Gollnick and Chinn, 1990). These examples of systematic planning instruments available for college teachers are not intended to be

Figure 2.4 Degree of Direct Student Involvement in Various Teaching Methods

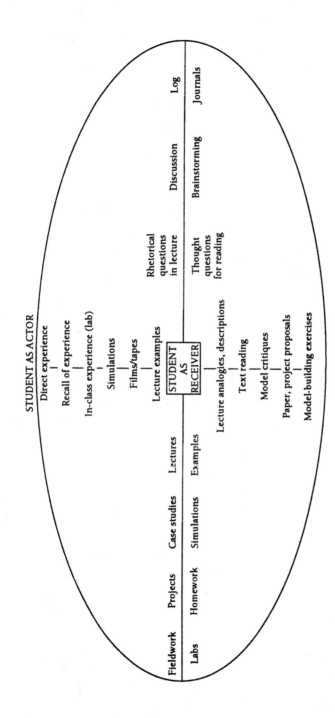

Source: Svinicki and Dixon, 1987, p. 146. Reprinted with permission of The Helen Dwight Reid Educational Foundation. Published by Heldreth Publications, 4000 Albermarle Street, NW, Washington, D.C. 20016. Copyright © 1987.

Figure 2.5. Substitute Vertical Continua Suggested by Multicultural Learning Orientation

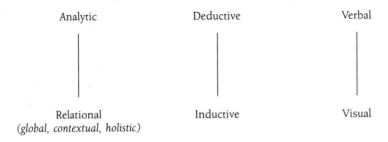

Analytic	Deductive	Verbal
Relational	Inductive	Visual
(global, contextual, holistic)		

Figure 2.6. Substitute Horizontal Continua Suggested by Multicultural Learning Orientation

Achievement Motive ———————— **Affiliation Motive**
intrinsic rewards   extrinsic rewards
                            (family, peers, community)

Competitive Mode ———————— **Collaborative Mode**
student vs. student   student with student

Separate ———————— **Connected**
student to student   student with student
teacher to student   teacher with student
information discretely   information in context
presented

exhaustive; other generative ideas appear in the gender and race ethnography literature (see Adams, this volume) and in the social justice training, problem- and contradiction-posing, and human relations training literatures (Weinstein, 1988; Jackson, 1976; Friere, 1970; Pfeiffer and Jones, 1974). Still other generic instructional design models are in the student development literature referred to earlier in connection with gender.

There is an emerging consensus that the repertoires of teaching strategies most effective and responsive in a socially and culturally diverse college classroom are the very same strategies that were identified at an earlier time as characteristic of teaching excellence for traditional students (Green, 1989). Many institutions have teaching and learning centers, where faculty members can continually develop, practice, and adapt their instructional approaches. Such centers operate under some model or set of assumptions about effective teaching. Some models identify and teach instructional skills in isolation, while others allow the instructor to explore efficacy relative to the skills, assets, needs, and characteristics of the students who are being taught. This latter approach suggests that there is no single normative model of teaching and learning and is therefore more appropriate for diverse student populations. For example, collaborative learning has been documented as an effective technique that can be applied to a variety of situations (Sheridan, Byrne, and Quina, 1989). However, MacGregor (1990) suggests that collaborative learning will become most effective when we reframe the student and teacher roles, which requires insight into the values, beliefs, behaviors, and styles of both the instructor and the learner.

One way to ascertain the degree of movement toward teaching efficacy is to examine the characteristics of excellent teachers who are associated with successful programs for diverse students. In general, these excellent teachers are likely to possess the following characteristics: (1) They assess their own strengths and weaknesses. (2) They tend to be student-centered. (3) They possess a repertoire of alternate teaching strategies. (4) They provide perspectives that reflect a respect for diverse views. (5) They are well prepared and organized. (6) They use techniques that encourage independent and critical thinking. And (7) they develop and utilize interpersonal skills that motivate students and facilitate learning.

These characteristics of effective instructors not only are important for interactions with diverse students but also are associated with teaching excellence for all students. Few instructors can be expected to exhibit all such characteristics, but, again, student success seems to correlate highly and incrementally with the increasing presence of these factors in the classroom. It is up to individual departments, deans, and provosts to provide the types of incentives that foster the enhancement of instructional competencies. These incentives must also be tied to a system of merit such that departments, and especially individual instructors, are rewarded within the context of professional development.

The movement toward diversity in higher education spans a broad spectrum of possible instructional interventions. An institution of higher learning can focus on many different aspects of instructional design but must ultimately come back to the classroom. The relationship between teaching and learning is now being reexamined through a more powerful magnifying glass. As diversity becomes a more significant concern, our attention will inevitably turn to how we can maximize the performance of diverse students in the classroom. Within this framework of inquiry and assessment, we shall find that as instructors broaden their repertoire of skills, greater numbers of traditional and nontraditional students will benefit from an enriched experience.

References

Anderson, J. "Cognitive Styles and Multicultural Populations." *Journal of Teacher Education,* 1988, 39 (1), 2–9.

Baker Miller, J. *Toward a New Psychology of Women.* (2nd ed.) Boston: Beacon, 1986.

Banks, J. "Teaching Assistants and Cultural Diversity." In J. Nyquist (ed.), *Preparing the Professoriate of Tomorrow to Teach.* Dubuque, Iowa: Kendall/Hunt, 1991.

Baxter Magolda, M. B. "Gender Differences in Cognitive Development: An Analysis of Cognitive Complexity and Learning Styles." *Journal of College Student Development,* 1989, *30* (3), 213–220.

Baxter Magolda, M. B. "Gender Differences in Epistemological Development." *Journal of College Student Development,* 1990, *31* (4), 555–561.

Carter, R. T. "Cultural Value Differences Between African Americans and White Americans." *Journal of College Student Development,* 1990, *31* (1), 71–79.

Claxton, C. S., and Murrell, P. H. *Learning Styles: Implications for Improving Educational Practices.* ASHE-ERIC Higher Education Reports, no. 4. Washington, D.C.: Association for the Study of Higher Education, 1987.

Condon, J. C. "The Ethnographic Classroom." In J. M. Civikly (ed.), *Communicating in College Classrooms.* New Directions in Teaching and Learning, no. 26. San Francisco: Jossey-Bass, 1986.

Cooper, G. "Black Language and Holistic Cognitive Style." *Western Journal of Black Studies,* 1981, *5,* 201–207.

Cross, K. P. *Adults as Learners: Increasing Participation and Facilitating Learning.* San Francisco: Jossey-Bass, 1987.

Friere, P. *Pedagogy of the Oppressed.* New York: Seabury Press, 1970.

Gelwick, B. P. "Cognitive Development of Women." In N. J. Evans (ed.), *Facilitating the Development of Women.* New Directions for Student Services, no. 29. San Francisco: Jossey-Bass, 1985.

Gilligan, C. *In a Different Voice: Psychological Theory and Women's Development.* Cambridge, Mass.: Harvard University Press, 1982.

Gilligan, C. "Remapping the Moral Domain: New Images of Self and Relationship." In C. Gilligan, J. V. Ward, and J. M. Taylor (eds.), *Mapping the Moral Domain: A Contribution of Women's Thinking to Psychological Theory and Education.* Center for the Study of Gender, Education, and Human Development, no. 2. Cambridge, Mass.: Harvard University Press, 1988.

Gollnick, D. M., and Chinn, P. C. *Multicultural Education in a Pluralistic Society.* New York: Merrill, 1990.

Green, M. F. (ed.). *Minorities on Campus: A Handbook for Enhancing Diversity.* Washington, D.C.: American Council on Education, 1989.

Hale-Benson, J. E. *Black Children: Their Roots, Culture, and Learning Styles.* (Rev. ed.). Baltimore, Md.: Johns Hopkins University Press, 1986.

Jackson, B. W. "Black Identity Development." In L. Golubschick and B. Persky (eds.), *Urban Social and Educational Issues.* Dubuque, Iowa: Kendall/Hunt, 1976.

Kluckhohn, F. R., and Strodtbeck, F. L. *Variations in Value Orientations.* New York: Harper & Row, 1961.

Kochman, T. *Black and White Styles in Conflict.* Chicago: University of Chicago Press, 1981.

Kolb, D. A. "Learning Styles and Disciplinary Differences." In A. W. Chickering and Associates (eds.), *The Modern American College: Responding to the New Realities of Diverse Students and a Changing Society.* San Francisco: Jossey-Bass, 1981.

Kolb, D. A. *Experiential Learning: Experience as the Source of Learning and Development.* Englewood Cliffs, N.J.: Prentice Hall, 1984.

Kuk, L. "Perspectives on Gender Differences." In L. V. Moore (ed.), *Evolving Theoretical Perspectives on Students.* New Directions for Student Services, no. 51. San Francisco: Jossey-Bass, 1990.

Lesser, G. "Cultural Differences in Learning and Thinking Styles." In S. Messick (ed.), *Individuality in Learning.* San Francisco: Jossey-Bass, 1976.

MacGregor, J. "Collaborative Learning: Shared Inquiry as a Process of Reform." In M. D.

Svinicki (ed.), *The Changing Face of College Teaching.* New Directions for Teaching and Learning, no. 42. San Francisco: Jossey-Bass, 1990.

Messick, S. "Personality Consistencies in Cognition and Creativity." In S. Messick (ed.), *Individuality in Learning.* San Francisco: Jossey-Bass, 1976.

Moore, C. "The Implication of String Figures for American Indian Mathematics Education." *Journal of American Indian Education,* 1988, 28 (1), 16–25.

Pearson, C. S., Shavlick, D. L., and Touchton, J. G. (eds.). *Educating the Majority: Women Challenge Tradition in Higher Education.* New York: American Council on Education/Macmillan, 1989.

Pfeiffer, J. W., and Jones, J. E. (eds.). *Handbook of Structured Experiences for Human Relations Training.* Vols. 1 and 2. (Rev. ed.) La Jolla, Calif.: University Associates, 1974.

Ramirez, M., and Castaneda, A. *Cultural Democracy, Bicognitive Development, and Education.* New York: Academic Press, 1974.

Ramirez, M., and Price-Williams, D. R. "Cognitive Style of Three Ethnic Groups in the U.S." *Journal of Cross-Cultural Psychology,* 1974, 5 (2), 212–219.

Rodgers, R. F. "Recent Theories and Research Underlying Student Development." In D. G. Creamer and Associates (eds.), *College Student Development Theory and Practice for the 1990s.* Alexandria, Va.: American College Personnel Association, 1990.

Shade, B.J.R. (ed.). *Culture, Style, and the Educative Process.* Springfield, Ill.: Thomas, 1989.

Sheridan, J., Byrne, A. C., and Quina, K. "Collaborative Learning: Notes from the Field." *College Teaching,* 1989, 37 (2), 49–53.

Smith, D. M., and Kolb, D. A. *User's Guide for the Learning Style Inventory: A Manual for Teachers and Trainers.* Boston: McBer, 1986.

Svinicki, M. D., and Dixon, N. M. "The Kolb Model Modified for Classroom Activities." *College Teaching,* 1987, 35 (4), 141–146.

Tharp, R. G. "Psychocultural Variables and Constraints: Effects on Teaching and Learning in Schools." *American Psychologist,* 1989, 44 (2), 349–359.

Weinstein, G. "Design Elements for Intergroup Awareness Training." *Journal for Specialists in Group Work,* 1988, 13, 96–103.

Witkin, H. A., and Moore, C. A. *Field-Dependent and Field-Independent Cognitive Styles and Their Educational Implications.* Princeton, N.J.: Educational Testing Service, 1975.

JAMES A. ANDERSON is professor of psychology at Indiana University of Pennsylvania.

MAURIANNE ADAMS is lecturer in human development, faculty in the Social Justice and Diversity Education Project, and director for Instructional Development and Social Issues Education (Residential Academic Programs) in the School of Education, University of Massachusetts, Amherst.

Achieving the truly multicultural classroom requires far more than admitting a diverse student population. Faculty must bring about nothing short of a transformation of academic culture.

Stirring It Up: The Inclusive Classroom

Jonathan Collett, Basilio Serrano

The demographic forecasts are clear: Previously underrepresented racial and ethnic groups will make up an increasingly large portion of the pool of potential students in higher education. In response, college and universities across the country have raised the banner of multiculturalism. Rural, mostly white institutions send recruiters to large urban high schools and arrange special visits of underrepresented students to their campuses. "Minority" faculty are courted at professional conferences. New courses exploring issues of gender, race, and class have appeared in college catalogues. It is the American Dream come true, the melting pot in action, with higher education leading in the effort to include those students previously excluded from the mainstream of American life.

The Limits of Inclusion

But day-to-day reality is not so encouraging to individual students. "Inclusion into whose world and on whose terms?" students ask. So far, very few of them have made their way into the mainstream. Only 30.3 percent of African-American and 32.3 percent of Latino students attain a college degree, compared to 55.8 percent white and 49.8 percent Asian-American students, according to a recent American Council on Education report (Carter and Wilson, 1991). Campus culture in the dorms and the student union is still predominantly middle class and white. Courses relating to women and marginalized groups are still peripheral, with faculty typically guarding against the dilution of a curriculum devoted to the best in the West. And perhaps the most subtle and most alienating phenomenon is that most American students attend traditional public schools and have

similar classroom experiences, yet many nonmainstream students experience the college and university culture as very different from their respective home community cultures.

Important questions persist as we move to the culturally, racially, and
gender-mixed classrooms that are inevitable in the next decade. What
numbers are required to form a critical mass of any one group so that
inclusiveness is not merely tokenism? How do we ensure that underrepresented groups experience inclusion as a time of swimming and not drown-
ing in their new academic culture? How do we accomplish inclusion of
these groups without a loss of their cultural identities? To what extent do
we accept the challenges raised by underrepresented students and faculty
to the traditional culture of the academic world? Are we willing to accept
ad hoc groupings by gender, race, culture, and sexual preference that
reinforce cultural identity and teach survival skills in a basically foreign
academic environment?

The Lessons of Separate Learning: Institutions and Programs That Build on Cultural Tradition

We can learn much about the ingredients of academic success for women,
African Americans, Latinos, and other groups by looking at the experience
of institutions where they have been either the sole constituency or in the
vast majority. At the same time that their numbers decrease and their financial resources dwindle, women's and traditionally black colleges have been
shown to foster academic and postgraduate accomplishment superior to
what these student groups have achieved in mixed institutions (Tidball,
1989; Fleming, 1984). Similarly, new research on the academic progress of
students whose native language is not English reveals that a strong grounding
in the native language, rather than placement in an all-English program,
results in greater academic success (Cummins, 1981, 1986). Common factors
account for the relative success of students in these separate experiences: a
supportive atmosphere, respect for cultural identity, high expectations, positive role models, and vigilance against bias. A brief look at these experiences
should be informative as we try to fashion multicultural campuses that work
for all men and women of all racial and ethnic groups.

Women's Colleges. When women students at Mills College launched
the strike in spring 1990 that led the trustees to rescind the decision to go
coeducational, they had done their homework. They cited studies to show
that graduates of women's colleges have been measurably more successful
after college than those from coeducational institutions. Although only a
small number of women's colleges are highly selective in admissions cri-
teria, graduates from these colleges are at least twice as accomplished in
future careers as women graduates from coed colleges. As Tidball (1989,
pp. 157–158) has observed, "The women's college story is one of nurture,

caring, discipline, high expectations, and appropriate rewards." These colleges also have more women faculty and administrators as potential role models.

In coed classes, women often find it more difficult to be recognized, are interrupted more, have their comments ignored with greater frequency, and find their ideas credited to men who raise similar points in discussion (Sandler and Hall, 1986). These difficulties are also common to male African-American and Latino students as well as those from other underrepresented groups. Women, however, comprise a majority in higher education, and so tokenism cannot be an excuse. The burden has been on women faculty and administrators as well as on women students (often from women's studies programs and women's centers) to change conditions in coed colleges and universities. What women study, how learning proceeds in the classroom, and how the quality of interactions in the campus community affects women are primary areas of concern.

Traditional Black Colleges. The experience of African-American students in traditional black colleges closely parallels that of students in women's colleges. Despite limited resources, black colleges provide their students with the kind of supportive atmosphere that leads to social and intellectual growth. These colleges help students clarify their group identity while fostering a positive self-image, a key combination for success. This is also the purpose of Native American tribal colleges, started largely in the 1970s because Indian students were not finding the support needed and were therefore often unsuccessful in mainstream institutions. But tribal colleges are now experiencing a funding crisis, as federal funds to support them were severely cut during the 1980s (Wright and Tierney, 1991).

The differences between a predominantly white and a predominantly black campus are felt most acutely by African-American male students. In her exclusive study of these contrasts, Fleming (1984, p. 142) describes the experience of black males in white colleges: "They become unhappy with college life. They feel that they have been treated unfairly. They display academic demotivation and think less of their abilities. They profess losses of energy and cease to be able to enjoy competitive activities."

On black campuses, however, black males show the same kinds of gains that white males achieve on white campuses. For African-American women the picture is more mixed. In black colleges they tend to blunt their assertiveness around African-American men and thus usually set lower goals for themselves (Fleming, 1984). This pressure to be more passive is somewhat reduced in white colleges, especially those located in the South. But the overall frustration of black women with the lack of support in white colleges reduces the higher education experience for many to an effort to survive.

Fleming (1984, p. 153) makes the important point that black colleges need not promote segregation but indeed are more likely to "serve as a stepping-stone for those who wish to become part of the larger society." Faculty and staff at black institutions are far more integrated than at white schools, allowing African-American students the opportunity to work through racial tensions in a more protected environment, with diverse role models.

Bilingual Education. A similar case against premature inclusiveness can be made from recent experience with bilingual education programs. Evidence shows that non-English speakers whose primary language is reinforced do better in English language skills than do those placed prematurely in an English-only program (Cummins, 1981, 1986). The key seems to be that proficiency in the native language entails conceptual guides to the underlying structure of the second language, English. Students can more easily add idioms, pronunciation, and other features of the surface syntactic structure of the new language when they have an understanding of the language's deep semantic structure (Cummins, 1981). Conversely, a non-native speaker can attain a surface fluency that is not sufficient for academic work. A teacher not skilled in recognizing the stages of language acquisition may attribute the student's failure to causes other than linguistic barriers.

Social factors are also important in language development, as in other learning skills: The nature of the communication with adults in the home is more critical to academic success than is the language in which this communication takes place. Strong cultural identity and use of language are important to success in English (Cummins, 1981).

To show some of the clear advantages of separate education for women, African Americans, those from language minorities, and others is not to argue that we give up on efforts to create mixed campuses. It is, however, to suggest that multicultural education on these campuses is currently failing to a large extent to address the needs of many students. The worst problem is the resistance and inability of predominantly white male faculty to recognize and respect gender and cultural differences among their students. The assumption that all students are the same, when they are not, most hurts nontraditional students. Rather than requiring an increasingly diverse student population to adapt to an existing culture that is fundamentally dissimilar to their own, faculty would do well to allow academic culture to change and be enriched by new perspectives and styles. Johnnetta Cole, president of Spelman College, explains the transformative goal in a statement that became the epigram for the 1991 national conference of the American Association of Higher Education: "We are for difference. For respecting difference. For allowing difference. Until difference doesn't make any more difference" (American Association for Higher Education, 1991).

Forms of Bias in the Classroom

Failure to be inclusive or to respect differences is manifested in many forms of bias. Bias in the classroom can be either outright prejudice that is readily detectable or a very subtle form that is not clearly identified either by the agent or recipient. Perhaps most violent is bias involving physical confrontation and corporal punishment. For example, there are continuing reports of ethnic minority school children who are physically punished for speaking their native languages in the classroom (Cummins, 1981). The most subtle bias may be manifested merely in the way a teacher looks at a student who speaks with a pronounced accent.

In actuality, identification of racial, ethnic, cultural, gender, or other kinds of bias in the classroom is usually not easy. The problem is that we all suffer from cultural blinders. A case in point is personal names, which vary in linear arrangement across cultures and have different social meanings. For example, names in some Asian cultures are organized in the reverse order of Anglo-American practice. For most Latinos both the mother's and father's surnames are important, yet it is somewhat insulting to use just the maternal surname that follows the paternal. Thus, Roberto Diaz-Cintron is properly addressed as either Mr. Diaz-Cintron or Mr. Diaz, but not as Mr. Cintron (Vazquez, 1970). It can be equally offensive for an instructor to anglicize a student's name. For example, Consuelo, if changed to Connie, may cause a breakdown in communication, even though the instructor intended no harm and was ignorant of the significance of the change.

Cultural Continua

Most students in the United States are participants in a transcultural experience that makes generalizations about cultural groups difficult to apply to individual students. In fact, as depicted in Figure 3.1, the degree of transculturation can be placed on a continuum with cultural experiences clearly embedded in a home culture at one end and a mainstream culture at the other. The degree of transculturation is complicated by the degree of English language proficiency possessed by the student. A second continuum of proficiency in English can be visualized. It is instructive to consider students, particularly if English is their second language, in terms of these two continua. For Latino students, for example, the horizontal continuum establishes the degree to which a student functions within Latin or Euro-American culture, and the vertical continuum establishes the degree to which the student is proficient in English.

Applying this grid to Latinos, we can see that the students in greatest need of culturally charged instructional approaches in an English language classroom are those in quadrant B, that is, students who are primarily Latin American in tradition (culturally embedded) and who are also primarily Spanish speakers. In contrast, women who are proficient speakers of English but share a nonmainstream culture that stresses collaborative learning and connected knowing modes are in quadrant A. Students with the least need for this type of intervention are those in quadrant D. These students

Figure 3.1. Transcultural and Language Proficiency Continua

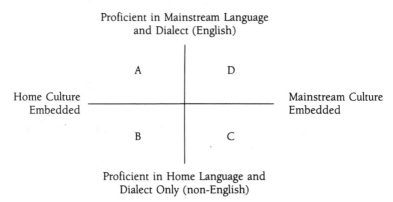

Proficient in Mainstream Language
and Dialect (English)

A   D

Home Culture   Mainstream Culture
Embedded   Embedded

B   C

Proficient in Home Language and
Dialect Only (non-English)

would likely experience difficulties in nontraditional classrooms. For example, a white male student who falls in quadrant D may need assistance in adjusting to collaborative or noncompetitive classrooms. Reduction or elimination of bias in instruction by responding to the cultural and linguistic characteristics that students bring to the classroom allows all students to recognize and appreciate their differences as well as their similarities.

Instructional approaches for effective teaching require that we consider where along the continua students are located. In the African-American community, for example, a salient dimension is the relative authoritarian versus democratic (but not laissez-faire) mode of the teacher (Delpit, 1988). An authoritarian approach may be favored by both students and teachers of the African-American community, with the more democratic approach seen as Euro-American and middle class. On the other hand, Little Soldier (1989) explains that Native American students are accustomed to making decisions on their own, without the imposition of adult authority. Therefore, an effective instructor is one who considers the cultural-linguistic modalities of all students.

Another application of these cultural continua involves the way that students are accustomed to determining what makes an idea valid. African-American college students, according to Kochman (1981), consider it essential for individuals to have personal positions on issues or ideas that they discuss in class and to assume full responsibility for arguing their validity. Euro-American students, on the other hand, see their basic role as reporting objectively on issues or ideas whose validity has been established by authorities in the field. African Americans in this scenario would view their contenders as trying to avoid the responsibility of taking a position. Euro-American teachers and students might feel the debate getting personal, nonintellectual, and thus out of control. Rodriguez (1988) suggests that Latino students may react in a way that is similar to their African-American counterparts, again depending on their positions along the cultural continuum.

Underrepresented students today are more likely to come in greater numbers from the barrio or ghetto (Saufly, Cowan, and Blake, 1983). These home cultures may make students' integration into higher education even more difficult since differences attributable to socioeconomic level may be added to differences of gender, racial, and ethnic background. Consequently, predominantly white, male faculty must gain a better understanding of the economic and cultural backgrounds of these students, which differ from American middle-class, mainstream culture. But it is also important that faculty not stereotype students. For many students, the requirements of negotiating two worlds—their respective home cultures and a mainstream culture that determines jobs and schooling—have forced a dual socialization. Depending on the degree of upward mobility emphasized in families and in previous schooling, some may be fully able to manage the dominant Euro-American values favored in most college classrooms (Hale-Benson, 1986).

The use of the previously mentioned continua need not be applied to students alone. Faculty can locate themselves along the continua. They can train themselves to move away from their own points of cultural embeddedness so as to communicate better with students and colleagues at other points along the continua. For example, an educator who decides to learn Spanish to better understand students who speak that language will be less likely to ask a student the often offending question, "Is English your native language?" Having developed an understanding of the phonemic structure of the Spanish language, the faculty member would know if the student is uttering English-language vocabulary with Spanish sound patterns.

If the goal of multicultural education is truly for students to learn the skills necessary to function effectively in the mainstream culture while maintaining their own cultural identities, faculty must understand these cultural continua and be able to identify where they and their students are placed. Avoidance of cultural issues under the guise of treating everyone alike is no longer acceptable. Faculty must, for example, confront problems of first-language interference among Asian students who are highly motivated to graduate yet have become skillful at circumventing writing-intensive courses and enlisting faculty complicity in their avoidance of language problems (Lou, 1989). Partial, generalized knowledge of culturally diverse groups in the United States is not enough if effective change in the way that faculty approach the inclusive classroom is to be achieved. Liberal, well-intentioned strategies, if based on insufficient understanding, may have negative results.

In a recent case at the State University of New York's College at Old

Westbury, one Latino student was advised by a Latino faculty member to improve writing skills in the English language. The student spoke with a subtle Spanish accent. After attending writing tutorials and after receiving much help from faculty, the student's writing did not improve. Since the faculty member in question was familiar with the literature on second-language acquisition, he began to suspect that the student's problem involved more than just written language skills. Furthermore, the student had been educated exclusively in New York and did not have a good command of Spanish. The faculty member had the student tested for a learning disability, which turned out to be the real problem. A well-inten-tioned but uninformed faculty member may have concluded that the prob-lem was simply the result of second-language acquisition and moved the student on to the next level with a low, but passing grade.

To summarize, it is important for faculty to consider where students are within the acculturation process and to adopt a varied, flexible teaching design that enhances learning for all. To go one step further, faculty may seek to become students of the new culture(s) that they are experiencing in the classroom. Through an immersion process similar to what many stu-dents experience, faculty can acquire the cultural knowledge needed to improve communication and teaching effectiveness.

Strategies for Genuine Inclusiveness

Making all students feel welcome, fostering their academic success, and embracing many cultural perspectives can be achieved through a variety of ways, including establishing a supportive climate, striving for curricular inclusiveness, and varying instructional strategies.

Extracurricular Activities. Campuswide activities can provide the kind of supportive climate necessary for women and underrepresented students to feel at home. Most important is a freshman program focusing on the transition from high school to college. Traditional orientation programs are a series of activities designed for students who are already well prepared for the culture of college. To support a multicultural student body, orientation programs must refocus and introduce the values and skills expected of successful college stu-dents to those students who are unfamiliar with these expectations.

Beginning with intensive summer sessions and continuing as a course during the fall semester, inclusive orientation programs stress training in study skills and a knowledge of college resources. But their most significant contribution may be in creating an awareness of cultural values appropriate to a college setting. Student behavior that may have been required to avoid physical abuse in an inner-city high school, for example—males wearing their pants down around their hips without a belt or never carrying their books on the street—can now be shown to be detrimental to college and career success.

In regular freshman courses, faculty must reinforce the same academic skills featured in the orientation course rather than assume that all students have been trained in note taking and summary and analysis skills. Faculty are the primary representatives of the new college culture emphasized in freshman programs and must be committed to joining their student development associates in planning and implementing orientation programs. In addition, workshops to orient faculty are needed to make them aware of the varying levels of student readiness and of the typical forms of bias in which they may unconsciously engage.

Peer relationships that lead to what is called *constructed knowing* are essential in the learning process (Belenky, Clinchy, Goldberger, and Tarule, 1986). Colleges should encourage a network of formal and informal activities that support student interaction both in and out of the classroom. Where a substantially large number of students of a particular cultural group is present, it is essential that organizations be started and occasions found for these students to work together on the issues facing them. Formal structures—cultural or racial fraternities and sororities, single-group dorms or houses, culture-based student organizations sponsoring discussions or a Black History or Women's History month—that already play an important role could do even more in the effort to retain students. Faculty and staff can, where possible, initiate library displays or film series on various cultural groups in conjunction with curricular offerings.

Informal approaches—performances by visiting artists, rap sessions in the dorms, cultural evenings or festivals—are possible even when small numbers of particular groups cannot support a full organization. Religious, business, and other community leaders, even in a city some distance from a rural college, can be called on to provide activities for students of their own particular cultural groups. The practice of opening campuses to broader community involvement not only benefits underrepresented students but also helps mainstream students and faculty to become more sensitive to the interests, traditions, and behavioral styles of local groups.

Course Planning. Teaching in the multicultural classroom is more than getting non-English names straight, using small groups, and adding a few women authors or non-Western texts to the syllabus. Good teaching has always had a single goal, student learning. In the inclusive classroom, attainment of this goal means significant changes in the way that courses have traditionally been designed and taught. The aim is not to emphasize deficiencies but rather to build bridges to students' existing knowledge and experience and to draw on their existing skills to move them forward.

With 90 percent of full-time faculty white and 72 percent male (82 percent of full professors are white and male!), the process of building two-way bridges from mainstream academic culture to an increasingly diverse student body is understandably difficult. The difficulty increases in the move up the status ladder from community colleges to research universities.

On the higher rungs of the ladder, nontraditional students decrease in number as a percentage of the student body and faculty are rewarded in inverse proportion to the effort that they expend in effective teaching. Academic disciplines almost exclusively determine the structure of the curriculum and faculty research. The task of progressing to truly multicultural curricula and classrooms, even for well-intentioned teachers, requires institutional and personal transformations because diversity challenges the structure of the disciplines as well as of the classroom.

Obviously, an individual course must be seen in the larger context of providing content and skills that students will need for a major, for more advanced courses, even for external certification in a profession. But taking these requirements into account, faculty should think carefully about the perspective that they wish to adopt in course content. Does the course view great Western thinkers and doers, usually males, as benchmarks of achievement in literature, philosophy, history, and the social and natural sciences? Are the contributions of women, racial and ethnic groups, non-Western cultures, or working-class people treated merely as exceptional cases that nevertheless must meet the standards of excellence laid down by the discipline (Green, 1988)? To judge texts in this manner is similar to treating all students in the class as homogeneous, with nontraditional students deserving recognition only if they succeed by the old, competitive, writing-intensive, analytical rules.

Incorporating the New Knowledge. The principal ingredient, therefore, for genuine inclusiveness is the integration of the so-called new knowledge, a euphemism used to identify previously devalued knowledge of women and ethnic and racial groups, into the overall curriculum and into specific courses (Bonilla and Gonzales, 1975). This integration must be genuine and not consist of mere add-ons to traditionally conceived knowledge. The more common approach is to use new knowledge sources to critique traditional ideas and models, as Gilligan (1982) does when she argues the limitations of prevailing theories of moral development that have failed to value the experience of women. A more difficult, but perhaps also even more effective, approach is for faculty to teach a subject from within the perspectives of women or underrepresented groups. As an example, for someone educated in Puerto Rico or other parts of Latin America, the Spanish-American War is normally referred to as the Cuban War of Independence. What is taught in Latin America about this conflict is different from what is taught in the United States. Along these lines, a whole course could be designed where the major events of a historical period are viewed through the eyes of, for example, a Cuban peasant or a medieval woman. This inside-out approach to an inclusive curriculum will clearly be difficult for faculty who are at or near the mainstream ends of the previously mentioned cultural continua.

Incorporation of new knowledge into the curriculum requires that faculty learn about the history and culture of women and men from working classes, different racial and ethnic groups, and other nationalities. A first step is to understand the use of certain basic terminology in order to avoid the kind of cultural prejudice that excludes important perspectives. For example, for Latin Americans the term *americanos* does not refer to the people of the United States but rather to the people of this hemisphere (the people of the United States are called *estadounidenses* or *norteamericanos*). People of the United States refer to the contiguous forty-eight states as the *mainland* in relation to the island of Puerto Rico, a term that neither Puerto Ricans nor other Latin Americans would use. To them, Puerto Rico is Puerto Rico; the United States is the United States, and there is no equivalent term for mainland in the Spanish language. Consideration of others' terminology requires at least a willingness to listen to the other side of the story.

The challenge, admittedly difficult, is to look for texts, films, and other course materials that question traditional ways of knowing along the same lines that multiculturally sensitive teaching questions traditional pedagogy. Several breakthrough books, although not necessarily appropriate as classroom texts, can serve as guideposts: Martin Bernal's (1987) *Black Athena,* Elizabeth Minnich's (1991) *Transforming Knowledge,* Stanley Fish's (1980) *Is There a Text in This Class?* and Bernardo Vega's (1984) *The Memoirs of Bernardo Vega: A Contribution to the History of the Puerto Rican Community in New York* are examples. The Feminist Press, Filmakers Films, Simile II (for educational simulations and games such as the innovative BAFÁ BAFA [Shirts, 1977] cross-cultural simulation) are representative of publishers and film and game distributors who make new kinds of classroom materials available.

Students can be asked to create texts for the class through oral histories or case studies of organizations in which they are involved. A business professor at the College at Old Westbury designed a marketing project where students used typical interviewing techniques to determine brand loyalty but were required to interview someone of their grandparents' generation. Students reported with great satisfaction that this assignment gave them their first opportunity to converse seriously with older people about the differences and similarities of values between generations. Although careful planning before the semester as to choice of texts, pace of semester, and course requirements is necessary, it is important to allow flexibility and be willing to change a syllabus once the particular cultural mix of the class is known.

Teaching Strategies. Teaching experts emphasize the importance of the first class meeting, and this claim is especially applicable to a classroom where inclusiveness is taken seriously. Sound objectives for the first class include taking time to pronounce names properly when the roll is called, obtaining information about items such as previous schooling and reasons for taking the course, and conducting an introductory ice-breaking exercise that engages students without demanding too much self-disclosure.

Understanding that nonmainstream students experience a cultural shift in the classroom, faculty can incorporate teaching strategies that draw on all students' learning modes. For example, a commonly held Latino belief is the preeminence of family and community. This belief is manifested by a need to protect family members and to be self-sacrificing (Fitzpatrick, 1987). A possible teaching strategy that is consistent with these practices is the use of collective, peer-teaching or student-teaming activities. This approach minimizes individualistic tendencies that are often frowned upon, even chastised, by Latinos. On the other hand, to prepare for and support the academic cultural shift that these students need to make, conventional strategies such as individual presentations and examinations should also be included in the course plan. The semester should feature a variety of teaching styles, providing support for the learning strengths of all students and nurturing alternative styles for those, including mainstream students, who have previously depended primarily on one style.

As the semester progresses, the faculty member should be attentive to opportunities for introducing to the class as a whole some relevant or currently important piece of information about various students' cultures. In one of our classes, for example, the effect of a hurricane in 1989 on a student who lost contact with his family in Jamaica became a matter of great concern to the whole class and the occasion for discussion about life in the Caribbean. The practice of taking time out of class to discuss current, especially controversial, issues, whether based on campus or world events, is characteristic of effective teachers, who support rather than detract from student academic development (Wilson and others, 1975).

Faculty should also find occasions for discussion of how cultural context influences what is taught and how it is taught. In addition to encouraging sensitivity about various cultural perspectives, these discussions make students aware of the learning process itself and their part in it (Collett, 1990). Instances occur when teachers or students use controversial terminology. One good example is use of the Spanish word *machismo*, which for mainstream English speakers automatically associates Latino males with the abuse of women. Nothing short of the elimination of the term may be required to remove this stereotype (Rivera, 1977).

Rather than highlight cultural phenomena that create conflict among various groups, faculty should accentuate what different groups have in common. For example, Irish, Latinos, and Italians all have a common religious tradition, which in turn defines common family-oriented practices. Latinos and African Americans share many religious, dietary, folkloric, and musical traditions. The role that women of all colors play in different cultures is also a potential avenue for cross-cultural understanding.

Conclusion

Student enrollments, much like the job market, will depend increasingly on the inclusion of large numbers of previously underrepresented groups. Higher education has to date been an inhospitable environment for these students; large numbers of them either do not graduate or do not perform up to their potential. Creation of the genuinely inclusive classroom requires the leadership of faculty who are willing to make major changes in an entrenched, traditional academic culture. These changes include an approach to teaching that combines personal caring with high expectations, an approach to content that incorporates new knowledge into the curriculum, and an authentic effort to understand and respond to the cultural perspectives of students and colleagues who come from outside the mainstream, Euro-American, white male culture that heretofore has characterized the academy. One starting point is for faculty to embark on significant "study abroad" trips to such places as the sovereign republic of El Barrio, the associated free state of Watts, or the domestic territory of the American Association of University Women.

References

American Association for Higher Education. Program. 1991 National Conference on Higher Education. Washington, D.C.: American Association for Higher Education, 1991.

Belenky, M. F., Clinchy, B. M., Goldberger, N. R., and Tarule, J. M. *Women's Ways of Knowing: The Development of Self, Body, and Mind.* New York: Basic Books, 1986.

Bernal, M. *Black Athena.* New Brunswick, N.J.: Rutgers University Press, 1987.

Bonilla, F., and Gonzales, E. "New Knowing, New Practice: Puerto Rican Studies." Centro working paper, Center for Puerto Rican Studies, Hunter College, New York, 1975.

Carter, D. J., and Wilson, R. *Ninth Annual Status Report: Minorities in Higher Education.* Washington, D.C.: American Council on Education, Office of Minorities in Higher Education, 1991.

Collett, J. "Reaching African-American Students in the Classroom." In L. Hilsen (ed.), *To Improve the Academy: Resources for Student Faculty and Institutional Development.* Vol. 9. Stillwater, Okla.: New Forums Press, 1990.

Cummins, J. "The Role of Primary Language Development in Promoting Educational Success for Language Minority Students." In Office of Bilingual Bicultural Education, California State Department of Education (ed.), *Schooling and Language Minority Students: A Theoretical Framework.* Los Angeles: Evaluation, Dissemination, and Assessment Center, California State University, 1981.

Cummins, J. "Empowering Minority Students: A Framework for Intervention." *Harvard Educational Review,* 1986, 56 (1), 18–36.

Delpit, L. "The Silenced Dialogue: Power and Pedagogy in Educating Other People's Children." *Harvard Educational Review,* 1988, 58 (3), 280–298.

Fish, S. *Is There a Text in This Class?* Cambridge, Mass.: Harvard University Press, 1980.

Fitzpatrick, J. *Puerto Rican Americans.* Englewood Cliffs, N.J.: Prentice Hall, 1987.

Fleming, J. *Blacks in College: A Comparative Study of Students' Success in Black and in White Institutions.* San Francisco: Jossey-Bass, 1984.

Gilligan, C. *In a Different Voice: Psychological Theory and Women's Development.* Cambridge, Mass.: Harvard University Press, 1982.

Green, M. F. (ed.). *Minorities on Campus: A Handbook for Enhancing Diversity.* Washington, D.C.: American Council on Education, 1989.

Hale-Benson, J. E. *Black Children: Their Roots, Culture, and Learning Styles.* (Rev. ed.) Baltimore, Md.: Johns Hopkins University Press, 1986.

Kochman, T. *Black and White Styles in Conflict.* Chicago: University of Chicago Press, 1981.

Little Soldier, L. "Cooperative Learning and the Native American Student." *Phi Delta Kappan,* 1989, *10,* 161–163.

Lou, R. "Model Minority? Getting Behind the Veil." *Change,* 1989, *21* (6), 15–17.

Minnich, E. K. *Transforming Knowledge.* Philadelphia: Temple University Press, 1990.

Rivera, M. "Machismo: Interplay of Sexual and Ethnic Stereotype." *Latin NY,* 1977, *2,* 40–41.

Rodriguez, C. *Puerto Ricans: Born in the U.S.A.* Boston: Hyman, 1988.

Sandler, B. R., and Hall, R. M. *The Campus Climate Revisited: Chilly for Women Faculty, Administrators, and Graduate Students.* Washington, D.C.: Project on the Status and Education of Women, Association of American Colleges, 1986.

Saufly, R. W., Cowan, K. O., and Blake, J. H. "The Struggles of Minority Students at Predominantly White Institutions." In J. H. Cones III, J. F. Noonan, and D. Janha (eds.), *Teaching Minority Students.* New Directions for Teaching and Learning, no. 16. San Francisco: Jossey-Bass, 1983.

Shirts, R. G. BAFÁ BAFÁ. (Copyright © 1977 by Simile II, 218 Twelfth Street, Box 910, Del Mar, Calif. 92014.)

Tidball, M. E. "Women's Colleges: Exceptional Conditions, Not Exceptional Talent, Produce High Achievers." In C. S. Pearson, D. L. Shavlik, and J. G. Touchton (eds.), *Educating the Majority: Women Challenge Tradition in Higher Education.* New York: American Council on Education/Macmillan, 1989.

Vazquez, J. "Understanding the Puerto Rican Child: The Puerto Rican Child in Puerto Rico." Communique to New York City Teachers, Board of Education of the City of New York, 1970.

Vega, B. *The Memoirs of Bernardo Vega: A Contribution to the History of the Puerto Rican Community in New York.* (C. A. Iglesias, ed.; J. Flores, trans.) New York: Monthly Review Press, 1984.

Wilson, R. C., Gaff, J. G., Dienst, E. R., Wood, L., and Baury, J. L. *College Professors and Their Impact on Students.* New York: Wiley, 1975.

Wright, B., and Tierney, W. G. "American Indians in Higher Education: A History of Cultural Conflict." *Change,* 1991, *23* (2), 11–18.

JONATHAN COLLETT is associate professor in the Comparative Humanities Program at the State University of New York, College at Old Westbury. He is founder and faculty coordinator of the Teaching for Learning Center, whose special focus is effective teaching and learning in college student populations that are diverse in age, class, race, and culture.

BASILIO SERRANO is associate professor of teacher education and director of bilingual teacher education at the State University of New York, College at Old Westbury. He is also chair of the board of directors of the Puerto Rican Heritage House in New York City.

The practice of raising teachers' awareness of their own inadvertent biases and presenting them with possible solutions encourages them to plan for equitable interactions in their classrooms.

Ensuring Equitable Participation in College Classes

Myra Sadker, David Sadker

> Like most university professors, I was a university student for many years. Most of my classes were concluded a few minutes before the bell—just in time for the professor to ask, "Are there any questions?" This was the discussion part of what was termed the lecture-discussion mode. To me those few minutes were often the most invigorating part of the class. Years later when I made the transition from student to professor, I considered a technique that would expand those last few minutes to the entire class period but would not dilute the content or diminish the intellectual challenge [Crow, 1980, p. 41].

As the professor's above comment suggests, interactive teaching goes beyond the lecture mode to actively involve students in their own learning. Students report that they enjoy participating in discussions more than they do sitting and listening to their professor talk for the entire period. Also, research makes it clear that interactive teaching is effective; when students participate in class, they are likely to achieve more and to have higher self-esteem.

For all of its benefits, interactive teaching has the potential for interjecting subtle bias into the college classroom. Studies analyzing classroom dynamics from grade school through graduate school show that teachers are more likely to interact with white male students. Elementary and secondary teachers ask boys more factual and analytical questions, give them more directions on how to accomplish tasks for themselves, and offer them more precise, clear feedback concerning the quality of their intellectual ideas. One three-year study of elementary and secondary schools found an interesting intersection of race and gender. The student most likely to be involved in classroom discussion was white and male. Minority males came in second in terms of teacher attention, while white females were third. The student least likely to be involved in discussion of intellectual content with the teacher and least likely to get time to talk was a minority female (Sadker, Sadker, and Klein, 1991).

In most cases, teachers want to be equitable in their distribution of attention. One reason that boys get more attention is that they grab it. They are eight times more likely than girls to call out answers and questions. While boys are involved in this active calling out, girls are more likely to sit with their hands raised, patiently waiting to be recognized. When boys call out, teachers accept and respond to their comments. When girls call out, teachers remind them, "Remember the rule, you're supposed to raise your hand in class" (Sadker, Sadker, and Klein, 1991). During this fast-paced classroom dynamic—with the teacher involved in as many as one thousand interactions a day—he or she is usually completely unaware of these inequities.

Studies of the postsecondary classroom also show that, compared to white males, all female students and minority males are more likely to be quiet in class and less likely to assume a powerful role in discussion (Sadker and Sadker, 1990). Like teachers in elementary and secondary school, most postsecondary instructors, regardless of gender, race, or ethnicity, report that they are completely unaware of these inequitable interaction patterns. If they are shown videotapes of their discussions or if a colleague comes into the class and systematically records interaction, they are often surprised to see patterns of subtle bias emerge. When they see these patterns, they want strategies to help them change.

Informal segregation, by race and ethnicity and/or by gender, also functions to intensify patterns of inequitable participation. If one analyzes the seating and group work patterns in multicultural, coeducational classrooms at any level of education, pockets of segregation become apparent; females sit with other females, and males cluster together. Approximately 50 percent of elementary and secondary classes are characterized by informal gender segregation, as are 30 percent of postsecondary classes. Similar seating clusters are evident for minority and majority students. While segregation is sometimes put in effect by the teacher, usually it is done by the students themselves. Rarely does the teacher intervene to integrate seating and group work, particularly in higher education.

When left intact, these segregated grouping patterns influence the distribution of teacher attention because the instructor is drawn to sections of the room where white males are clustered. Consequently, all females and minority males are out of the instructor's immediate visual zone. Literally invisible, they are less likely to be called on to participate, and so they become silent as well (Sadker and Sadker, 1990).

Ineffective use of wait time also plays a role in subtly encouraging male students to participate more. Wait time is the amount of silence that the instructor allows after asking a question and before a student responds. After asking a question, the teacher typically waits nine-tenths of a second for a student to answer. If the student answer is not forthcoming in that split second, the teacher either answers the question or calls on another student. If teachers can increase their wait time from less than one second to three to five seconds, especially when discussing complex and difficult subject matter, there are many positive benefits. Student achievement increases, especially on tests measuring complex levels of achievement; the discourse becomes more sophisticated; and more students voluntarily participate in class discussion, particularly those who are shy and more hesitant to respond.

While, in general, all students could benefit from more wait time, research shows that teachers give white male students a little more wait time than they do others. Wait time not only gives a student a little bit more time to think, but it is also a vote of confidence in that student. It says, "I have faith in your ability to answer the question, so I will give you more time to think about it" (Sadker and Sadker, 1990).

These subtle inequities in attention have an impact on student achievement (Sadker, Sadker, and Klein, 1991). According to standardized testing, starting from about the fourth grade, minority achievement begins a significant decline. While girls begin school equal to or ahead of boys in every academic area, by the time they graduate from high school they are behind boys in almost every academic area, especially math and science. This academic gender gap continues through higher education. Male students outperform female students on both verbal and mathematical sections of the graduate record exam as well as on exams such as the Medical College Admission Test (MCAT) and the Graduate Management Admissions Test (GMAT) requisite for entrance into professional schools of medicine and business, respectively.

Faculty Development Program for Equity in Instruction

Despite these discouraging findings, there is a positive side to the research. Our research shows that after participating in a carefully designed faculty development program, professors can eliminate inequitable instruction. With support from the Fund for the Improvement of Postsecondary Education, we created and evaluated an equity training program at the American University in Washington, D.C. (Sadker and Sadker, 1990). Twenty-three faculty from a dozen schools and departments throughout the university participated. Another twenty-three faculty members, matched by age, sex, race, and academic discipline, were the control group.

On the first day of the equity training program, faculty reviewed classroom interaction research and analyzed videotapes and live role plays to determine both overt and subtle bias. On the second day, the professors participated in a teaching clinic. They taught brief lessons in their academic discipline to college students who had volunteered to participate. The lessons were videotaped. Colleagues observed their teaching using a systematic observation instrument. They also gave feedback to the professor teaching the lesson and provided coaching on how to improve instruction for both equity and effectiveness.

This training program was unique; it asked professors not only to talk about teaching but also to practice it before their colleagues and give each other feedback about teaching strengths and areas in need of improvement. Faculty reacted positively. As one professor commented, "I've been teaching more than twenty years, and this is the first time a colleague ever watched me teach and talked with me about what I was doing."

Following the clinical equity program, trained raters visited the classrooms of the twenty-three professors who had received training, as well as the classes of the twenty-three faculty in the control group. The classrooms of all forty-six faculty were coded three times for a total of 138 fifty-five-minute observations during the course of one semester. There were significant differences between trained and control group faculty on a number of factors, including frequency and effectiveness of interaction and degree of bias.

In the typical control group classroom, male students dominated interactions. Ten percent of the students, usually male, were involved in 25 percent of the interactions with the professor. Almost half the students did not participate, even minimally, in the discussion; these silent students were usually female.

Trained faculty were 38 percent more interactive than their control group colleagues. They gave more precise and clear feedback to all students. Only seven percent of their students were silent. Females and males were equally active in classroom discussion.

Recommended Teaching Strategies

As a result of our two-year equity training project at the American University and the training sessions that we have conducted at institutions of higher education across the country, we suggest the following teaching strategies. If faculty can incorporate these research-based recommendations into their teaching, they will become more effective and more equitable.

Code the Class. The only way to determine the degree of equity in one's own classroom interactions is to get objective coding of the class. While our training sessions prepare college instructors to use a comprehensive coding instrument, there are several simpler techniques that provide faculty with important new insights into their teaching.

The simplest observation technique is a frequency count. Instructors ask a colleague or even a student in their classes to record each of their interactions with a student. Using a seating chart of the class that indicates the gender and race of each student, the instructor asks the observer to make a mark on the chart next to the name of each student who interacts with the instructor. It is important to record both students who volunteer (perhaps with a V) as well as students who are called on (perhaps with a line). It is best to rely on more than a single class observation, but two or three classes are usually representative of teaching behavior. This collection of data can open up a number of provocative teaching issues. Instructors should consider the following questions: How many interactions are there in the classroom? How many students do not participate in any interactions? Do any students dominate discussions? Does the instructor rely on volunteers or independently decide who will speak? Are there geographical areas of the class that receive considerable instructor attention? Are there other areas that are blind spots, where students receive little or no attention?

Gender, race, and ethnic differences can also be explored using this same data. After determining the proportion of males and females and various ethnic and racial groups in their classes, instructors should consider the following questions: Does the instructor call on females and males equitably, that is, in proportion to their attendance in the class? Does the instructor call on racial and ethnic minorities equitably? How many females or minority males are silent members of the class?

While it is useful for instructors to be aware of research findings concerning gender and race bias in classroom interaction, there is no substitute for objective records of what life in their classrooms is like. While there is a good chance that several of the national findings will apply to one's own teaching, there are likely to be differences as well. The more precise the knowledge of their own teaching, the more focused instructors can be in identifying strategies to improve their classroom practices.

Increase Wait Time. Although an instructor may not be aware of the length of his or her typical wait time, it is important to have a student or colleague determine the average amount of time between instructor questions and student responses. This measure can be taken by observing a few classes and timing the interlude between question and response with a stopwatch. Obviously, it is more important to use longer wait times after difficult questions are asked.

Although it is easy to learn about wait time, it is hard to incorporate this strategy into behavior. Some instructors have learned to increase wait time by actually counting to themselves for three to five seconds. In our research, one teacher explained that she actually puts her hand over her mouth and assumes a contemplative stance; this becomes an actual physical technique to remind her to wait longer and give students a chance to think before answering. Professors who can develop extended wait time will hear new voices in the classroom—especially those belonging to white women and people of color. Classroom discussion is enhanced by more thoughtful and more representative student participation.

Become an Intentional Teacher. In the workshops that we give for college faculty across the country, we repeatedly hear professors express frustration because the same few students in a class seem to answer all of the questions. Some instructors worry that it may be rude to deny the opportunity to speak for those who have a lot of good things to say. While it is useful, important, and polite to recognize volunteers, it is neither fair nor efficient to let these students dominate. To permit this domination is to abandon the instructor's role as a gatekeeper to classroom interaction and to reassign that role to whatever student or group of students happens to be the most loquacious. Such reassignment has deleterious effects, especially for the more reticent students who are likely to get shut out of the interaction. Research indicates that these quieter students are more likely to be racial or ethnic minorities and twice as likely to be female.

Some professors worry about calling on and possibly embarrassing quiet students who are not volunteering and who may even be avoiding attention and participation. While faculty should not humiliate quiet students, it is also important to encourage them to take an active role in discussion. Learning is not a passive activity and education is not a spectator sport. The teacher who makes the decision to engage silent students is intentionally sending the message that all students are expected to be active members of the class.

Desegregate Student Seating. When students are allowed to form seating clusters that consistently reflect gender and racial segregation, there are several negative consequences. Instructors are drawn to the white and male areas of the class; females and minority males are less likely to be seen and even less likely to be heard. Formal segregation without intervention sends to students unfortunate messages about separate societies and does little to prepare them for workplaces integrated by race and gender. Professors who have chosen to intervene have done so in a variety of ways. Some have students sit according to a seating chart. Others openly discuss with their students why those seating patterns may occur and the potential negative impact. Still other instructors integrate students by forming cooperative learning groups that are heterogeneous according to race, gender, and ability level.

Teaching Tactics. A number of professors have shared with us various techniques that they use to ensure equitable instruction.

Name Cards. Some instructors find it useful to put each student's name on three-by-five-inch index cards, shuffle the cards, and then call on each student as his or her name is drawn from the pile. This technique ensures both random and equitable participation.

Mobility. Walking around the classroom can give the instructor a new perspective, especially walking to the far corners or the back row of the class. Research shows that males are likely to be called on wherever they sit in the class, but females are more likely to participate if they sit close to the instructor. Movement around the class helps to ensure that the quieter students—minority men, white women, and women of color—are not allowed to be silent and invisible.

Poker Chips. One professor came up with a particularly creative idea. She distributed three poker chips to each student in her class. In order to talk, a student had to deposit a chip in the center of the room. Before the class ended, students were expected to spend all of their chips; but students were not allowed to talk after their chips were spent. This forced the garrulous students to think about their comments and filter significant comments from the trivial. Quiet students, on the other hand, had to think of something to say. The result was that all students were involved in the discussion.

Name Tags. A simpler technique that offers a start in promoting student participation is to ask each student to print her or his name on each side of a notebook page and to display it as a nameplate on the desk during each class. For some instructors, especially in large classes, just having a name to call on facilitates discussion and encourages the practice of calling on quieter students whose names may be forgotten.

Comment Cards. In this technique, each time a student provides a strong response or an insightful comment, the instructor hands the student an index card called a *comment card*. At the end of the class, the students who have received the cards come to the instructor and a notation is made next to their names on the class attendance list. Periodically, the instructor reviews the class list and encourages those students who have not earned any comment cards to increase their class participation.

Students are charged the same tuition whether they are invisible in class or whether they demand more than their fair share of their instructors' educational time and attention. To ensure that education is an equitable and inclusive process, carefully designed faculty development and training programs are essential. The research and recommendations discussed in this chapter are intended to provide a way to begin.

References

Crow, M. L. "Teaching as an Interactive Process." In Kenneth E. Eble (ed.), *Improving Teaching Styles.* New Directions for Teaching and Learning, no. 1. San Francisco: Jossey-Bass, 1980.

Sadker, M., and Sadker, D. "Confronting Sexism in the College Classroom." In S. Gabriel and I. Smithson (eds.), *Gender in the Classroom.* Champaign: University of Illinois Press, 1990.

Sadker, M., Sadker, D., and Klein, S. "The Issue of Gender in Elementary and Secondary Education." *Review of Research in Education.* Washington, D.C.: American Educational Research Association, 1991.

MYRA SADKER and DAVID SADKER are professors of education at the American University in Washington, D.C.

An examination of two feminist classrooms elucidates the instructors' and students' relationship to mastery, voice, authority, and positionality.

Inside Feminist Classrooms: An Ethnographic Approach

Frances Maher, Mary Kay Thompson Tetreault

The transformational impact of the last two decades of feminist scholarship on the academic disciplines and college curricula has been well documented. Feminist theorists and other postmodern scholars have shown us that all knowledge is a social construction and that the male-dominated disciplines have given us at best partial truths and at worst a discourse that silences or marginalizes other ways of knowing. Thus, feminist postmodernists have called attention to women's positions of oppression in society as sources of legitimate claims to truths, truths obscured heretofore by perceived universals based on the male experience. These theorists argue that only consciously partial perspectives such as those derived from women's various positions within society can guarantee the objectivity of knowledge, an objectivity based not on impartiality but on acknowledgement of particular contexts, experiences, and histories.

The pedagogical implications and classroom enactments of a developing feminist theory of knowledge are now being explored in an ethnographic research project done by the authors that systematically uses feminist theories to examine women as teachers, students, and knowers within the classroom context. Classroom pedagogies and the processes of knowledge construction that are emerging in the classrooms of feminist teachers are important topics to explore because they have wide-reaching implications for teaching and learning.

Feminist Pedagogies

Feminist teaching practices have emerged in the margins of and in sharp contrast to the practices of the traditional college classroom—a context marked by the rational critical discourse of positivism and the search for a single, universal, objective reality. There, students are expected to master materials and arguments and come to rational and objectively verifiable conclusions based on a falsely universal view of the world. At the heart of traditional pedagogy is the goal of mastery: an understanding of the truth of a work, what it really means, and thus an ability to dominate or control it the way that the authorities in the field have traditionally done. While the predominant mode of traditional teaching is lecturing, discussions also tend to aim, via the Socratic method or techniques of critical thinking, to overall generalizations that are meant to subsume or reconcile different points of view. One teacher captured the limitations of this form of teaching:

> I used to come into the classroom with a list of questions and I knew where they were leading. Very Socratic! I don't teach Socratically anymore. I think it's very manipulative. . . . I would get frustrated if the students didn't take the thing in the direction I thought they were supposed to . . . so I missed all these wonderful insights that they have to offer. They may not be able to develop such an insight in as sophisticated a way as you and I can, but they can sometimes come up with the absolute crucial starting point for a really interesting piece of interpretation, and the more they do it, the farther they can take it.

Another problem with traditional pedagogy is that it rewards learning that is associated with rational, objective approaches and as it happens, with male students. Frequently, the mark of success becomes the grade that a student achieves rather than the student's development of the ability to make meaning. Belenky, Clinchy, Goldberger, and Tarule (1986) have identified this requirement of mastery as a hallmark of separate, rather than connected, knowing, whereby students learn disciplinary content and methods of analysis on the terms of the dominant culture but forgo—especially in the case of women and minority students—a personal emergence that comes from connecting their education to their own experiences, or from raising and answering their own questions and concerns. One of our female student informants describes how mastery works and her resistance to it: "I went through years of school without saying a word because the professor would ask something and I'd know what he wanted to hear but I wouldn't tell him."

Feminist pedagogy was originally conceived as an alternative to these traditional pedagogical paradigms. Feminist pedagogy, culturally constituted and ascribed to women in general, has been defined as cooperative rather than competitive, attentive to student experiences, and concerned with the personal and relational aims and sources of knowledge. Its roots have been traced back to both the consciousness-raising groups that launched the women's movement (reframing *the personal is political* to *the personal is educational*) and the pedagogical practices associated with progressive, student-centered, and liberatory models of education.

Since the 1970s, there has been a growing literature on feminist pedagogy that has been useful to many teachers, but the work has been confined to self-reports and has come to seem overly prescriptive (Maher, 1985a, 1985b). The purpose of this chapter, therefore, is to summarize specific practices of two feminist teachers selected from a study of eighteen teachers in six different college environments. Their practices illustrate the wide variety of choices, conflicts, and creative possibilities faced in their classrooms. Here, we examine four issues: mastery of materials and what constitutes knowledge, student voice and identity, authority and the ways in which feminist teachers and students negotiate authority, and positionality, that is, the ways in which an individual's position in the classroom and in society affects learning.

Mastery, Voice, Authority, and Positionality

Our four major themes, *mastery, voice, authority,* and *positionality,* emerged from a complex combination of experience and reflection on data collected over several years of fieldwork. The themes evolved from transcripts of class discussions, conversations with informants, readings in feminist theory, and, finally, an examination of our own personal histories as students, feminist teachers, and feminist researchers over the past decade. (Our thinking about where learning, or mastery, is embedded has also benefited greatly from conversations with Jill Mattuck Tarule.)

Mastery has traditionally meant the goal of rational comprehension of material on the teachers' or experts' terms. In the feminist classrooms described in this chapter, students seek mastery on their own terms and in concert with others. Thus, individual mastery is embedded in the social construction of knowledge—it becomes collaborative, based on interaction among peers, rather than hierarchical. Rather than achieving rational comprehension of the material on the teachers' terms, students make increasingly more sophisticated connections with the topics. Universal notions of "the right answer" give way to notions of mastery as empowerment—an instrument for previously silenced students to "claim an education," to use Adrienne Rich's (1979) expression.

Voice has recently become a metaphor for the emergence of women's consciousness and experiences into the public sphere, symbolizing both personal awakenings and new visions of the world. For the classrooms that we studied, voice connotes the ways in which the students and teachers articulated their own sense of their experiences and their learning. It means speaking for oneself and bringing one's own questions and perspectives to the material. It connotes a connection of one's education to one's personal experience, a connection that women and other oppressed groups must often give up when they seek mastery on the terms of the dominant discourse of traditional pedagogy.

The third theme is that of authority. In traditional classrooms, teachers and students stand in a hierarchical relationship to knowledge and to scholarly expertise. The traditional teacher's authority comes from his or her role as interpreter of the knowledge of experts, who are believed to be closest to the ultimate truth of any event or idea. With new paradigms of knowledge construction that view truth as the product of multiple perspectives, feminist teachers must reevaluate the source and implications of their authority. The issue of authority then becomes problematic and challenges both teachers and students. Teachers see themselves as facilitators and resources, viewing their expertise as derived from their own individual and collective experience rather than from a superior access to truth. They also see their authority as grounded in their own diverse commitments as feminists, with necessarily partial but still legitimate worldviews.

Positionality encompasses recent feminist thinking about how the validity of knowledge comes from an acknowledgment of the knower's specific position in any context, as defined by gender, race, class, and other variables. Linda Alcoff (1988) calls for an acknowledgment of women's various societal positions as the sources of feminist perspectives, with the concept of positionality replacing a biologically determined essential woman; Sandra Harding (1987) attempts to locate and describe a female standpoint; and Donna Haraway (1988) describes what she calls "situated knowledges," whereby objectivity comes not from a false impartiality but from the acknowledgment of all perspectives as partial and particular. The concept of positionality, first articulated for us by one of our teacher informants, points to contextual and relational factors as crucial for defining not only our identities but also our knowledge as women teachers or students in any given situation. Feminist teaching practices reposition the relationships among teachers, their students, and their materials, producing an epistemological shift away from the teacher as the sole authority and transforming the students' experiences of mastery and voice.

In this chapter we present sketches of two professors' teaching practices in terms of their goals, their classroom techniques, and their students' experiences of the class. To illustrate the ways in which each teacher challenges the traditional classroom by pursuing alternative pedagogies and forms of knowledge construction, we analyzed their teaching in relation to the four themes described above using both classroom transcripts and interviews with the teachers and their students.

Mastery, Authority, and the Construction of Knowledge

We first came to the theme of mastery after observing Laurie Finke, an English professor at Lewis and Clark College in Portland, Oregon. On the first day of class, while introducing her course on literary theory, Finke stressed that students should immerse themselves in the material, jot down in journals questions that arise as they do the reading, and come to class to pool the information that they have gathered, rather than trying to be "master of whatever materials we are reading." This charge to her students to give up mastery in favor of immersion was a way of making them coinvestigators and equals in the exploration of topics in the classroom. She wanted them to construct their own relationships with the materials, to be as active as the instructor in relation to the issues that would be raised.

As the class progressed, discussions usually began with students presenting questions and answers from their journal entries, rather than with Finke's own questions on the material. By instructing the students to ask and answer their own questions, she established an alternative way of constructing knowledge and transformed the role of mastery as a goal of teaching and learning. The practice of beginning with the students' questions rather than with the teachers' is an important innovation in feminist classrooms. The anthropologist Shirley Brice Heath (1983) has observed how heavily teachers have been socialized into thinking that they should teach by asking questions.

In the classroom that we studied, rather than head toward a rational comprehension of the material on the teacher's and experts' terms, Finke sought to enable students to seek learning on their own terms and in concert with others, thus initiating a collective rather than hierarchical learning process. She suggested this goal of collaboration when she said, "And as we come together to pool that information we may come up with more definitive answers." She also wanted her students to feel that "they have equal access to the agenda of the day."

How did students experience this shift toward construction of a collaborative relationship with the material that asked them to recognize their own questions and their own voices? Because the course focused on theory rather than fictional narrative, several of the students were silenced in this class, feeling they could not easily attain the equal access that Finke sought for them. Carole, a traditional student who was preparing to teach high school English, seldom spoke in class. She felt that before she could interact with the materials and participate as an equal in the classroom, she had to "assimilate and understand the material," in short, master it in the traditional sense of that concept. She said, "It's hard for me to do what Laurie wants us to do and criticize it, because I'm just assimilating it, understanding it . . . so I have a hard time contributing. [Yet] it's a great experience. It's the most challenging class I ever had." When, in accordance with our desire to get our teacher informants' views of what was happening in their classrooms, we showed her quotes to the teacher, Finke pointed out that students who have seldom achieved mastery in traditional ways might be especially loath to abandon that approach.

Another student, Jane, who was twenty-eight years old at the time of these observations and also preparing to be a teacher, felt that Finke helped her move through conventional concerns about mastery to a rewarding awakening as she wrote a paper for the college's annual Gender Studies Symposium. Jane described the process this way: "My rough draft was a synthesis of feminist theory in general, but I didn't come up with anything new." Stuck there, she went to Finke, who said, "This one sentence [at the end] is great. It could be the beginning sentence. Start with that sentence and write." Anxiety stricken because her presentation was the next day, Jane went home and went to bed, got up at four o'clock in the morning and wrote until nine o'clock that morning. She reported, "It was all organized. I got up there and read it and it went real well."

The experiences of these two students suggest that it may not be enough to instruct some students, particularly females, to bring their own questions to the materials. They may first need some confirmation that their own concerns and identities are legitimate. The insight of Belenky, Clinchy, Goldberger, and Tarule (1986) that women are connected knowers suggests that many female students perceive themselves as having a subjective voice in relation to knowledge, not a separate, rational stance seeking objective truth. They need to make the material part of themselves, first, to assimilate it rather than master it.

Even though female students tended to be more silent than were the males in the class, the two male students that we interviewed talked more about *being* silenced in the class. The women-centered content of Finke's class put male and female students into a different relationship with the material. Male students may feel silenced in feminist classrooms because they are no longer the authorities and the dominant position of males in society is often in question. However, in Finke's class the males were also disturbed by the redefinition of mastery in her pedagogical approach.

The feminist practice of reconceptualizing the construction of knowledge as a collaborative effort did not lead male students to reflect on issues of mastery but rather on issues of authority. Two of the most talkative students, Ned and Robert, were more worried about their own positions vis-à-vis the other students and the teacher authority figure than their own development as learners. In courses with feminist teachers, they were taught to approach discussions in a more collaborative way, and they came to see their positions in these classes as problematic. Ned, the student who initiated the most topics for class discussion and who was a prominent debator on campus, appreciated Finke's democratic style but missed the old challenge of struggling with a dominant authority figure. He said, "I've been in classes where I've been encouraged to go after people. . . . If that class had consisted [of different students], we would have come closer to the level of Laurie's voice and I think we should have made her take back the power she relinquished. I think we would have made her take it back to defend it. . . . It wasn't a debate. There are plenty of people around here who would like to argue with an authoritative voice."

Comments such as these helped us to see authority as another of our major themes. Later in the interview, Ned acknowledged that he admired Finke for empowering students to approach the material with their own questions; yet he longed for combative discourse with an expert more powerful than he. Ned's desire for a debate also suggests, however, that he was still locked into the search for traditional mastery, for the ultimate truth of any event or idea, and into achievement through competitive struggle.

Robert, who was thirty-five years old and who referred to himself as a former member of Students for a Democratic Society, could be heard probing the relationship between gender and discourse when he said, "It's real easy to dominate, and I wouldn't want to do it [in Finke's class]. I mean I walk on eggshells." And Ned said, "If I were to try to be combative where I am one of six males in a class, in some ways I begin to replicate the problems of authority unintentionally. And you just don't want to set up that kind of situation." Both knew that class discussions often reproduce traditional gender relations with males as dominant, and yet they continued to be drawn to the traditional mode of discourse.

This examination of mastery and authority also entails an exploration of the various forms of authority contained in Finke's teaching role, as the expert, the resource, the evaluator, and the facilitator of discussion. How did she use her authority as the teacher to convey knowledge, to direct the course of discussion, and to encourage and to restrain the activities of different students? In the dialogue excerpts that follow, we present an example of an occasion where she engaged with the students as an equal participant and yet also used her expertise to resolve a dispute by explaining a difficult concept, the concept of positionality.

This class on literary theory was an extended discussion of the ideas of three prominent French feminists—Hélène Cixous, Luce Irigaray, and Julia Kristeva (Moi, 1985). Comparison of their views led the class to question the relationship between gender and social class, and Robert had initiated an extended discussion of this issue by arguing with Jane and a few others that economic oppression was more important than gender oppression. Finke maintained a nonauthoritarian position by going along with their choice of topic and did not direct the discussion for a long time. When the students finally seemed stuck around the issue of gender versus class as primary oppositions, she tried to resolve it by introducing the concept of positionality.

FINKE: What we need is a description that is not based on categories but, as Kristeva says, on positionality, on relations. In other words, in your example, although women generally are marginal in our culture, the example you give suggests a slightly different position in which the whole question of who is oppressed and who is central and who is marginal depends on its relation to what.

MARGARET: Well, who created it as the center?

FINKE: Well, no group is in and of itself oppressed or marginal. It's only in relation to something else. So that, for instance, women are marginal to men, but black women are marginal compared to white, middle-class women.

NED: And there's no margin without center.

FINKE: There's no center. We are falling into the whole androcentric trap of trying to find the center when what we need is to keep the whole model in motion.

(Later . . .)

MARGARET: One of the things I thought about when Kristeva was talking about marginality is that positioning relates to man, the center, . . . is going in a straight line. . . . I think that if Kristeva sort of went one step further, . . . [and] created not only the wedge she talks about in language but a web that goes beyond language. Because in a web a binary opposition doesn't really have a chance to survive.

FINKE: Right. Absolutely.

(Later . . .)

FINKE: Yeah, you begin to create a margin which then reinscribes the same center margin dichotomy itself and what you need to do is keep deconstructing that, keep seeing it as relational. Keep seeing it as position.

JANE: Do you think that there are ways in which this kind of approach or attitude can be dangerous for feminism in the sense that it sort of opens things up so that patriarchy can use that rationale to its advantage?

FINKE: How?

JANE: I don't know how. That's what I'm asking you guys. Do you think there is a possibility of that?

FINKE: I mean, I tend to.

SAM: [to Jane] It, isn't it sort of defusing the power of the movement sort of? Is that what you mean?

JANE: I don't know what I mean.

FINKE: That exactly comes from that mentality of seeing the women's struggle as being somehow divorced from the racial struggle or the class struggle. A relational kind of thing like this, I think, far from dividing and conquering, would encourage more cross-referencing across those different kinds of struggles. Instead of seeing them all as separate or all as the same struggle, you see a whole series of relationships. I mean, how does feminism keep from creating a white, middle-class feminist movement which is completely ignorant of what is happening in racial struggles or class struggles?

SAM: So, in other words, the division is going to be there and it's better to recognize them than to pretend they are not.

FINKE: Yeah.

(Later . . .)

JANE: [raises her point again] Your gender determines in some ways how much you can achieve, to some extent, I mean there is a tendency that way because of the binary opposition.

NED: I agree.

FINKE: But the fact is that all those things do. They all work together. You can't privilege one.

JANE: I'm using it as an example.

FINKE: Yeah, you can't privilege one over the other.

The discussion above focused on a collaborative exploration of the issues of gender, race, and class raised by the reading assignment, rather than a mastery of what the materials said. Even though Finke quoted Kristeva (or Moi, 1985), it was as if she were using the text to convey her own sense of the issues involved and her interpretation of them, rather than an authoritative final version. When she invoked the concept of positionality, she used it to resolve a dispute that several students had created. However, she was also using her authority as the teacher in a more subtle way. We thought that she was ignoring Jane's concern about the actual oppression of women in order to keep the theoretical relationships among different oppressions clear. Perhaps her teaching goal of "coming together to come up with more definitive answers" was brought into play here, as she pushed the students to a certain conclusion. And yet Jane hung in there, undaunted, so that the flavor was of an argument among equals rather than of the imposition of one view by the teacher.

Thus, in this excerpt, we see Finke both relinquishing and displaying her authority in several complex ways. She opened the discussion with students' questions rather than her own, and at many points she sat back in order to give the students full rein. When she did come in as the voice of expertise, she did so in order to resolve the dispute over whether women are a class. But even in this context, the students took her on and disputed her on the question of whether deconstruction (or positionality) is dangerous for feminism. Finke stated her position, and she did so at some length, but she expected and was challenged by student responses. In this excerpt, we see her definitions of mastery, namely, giving students equal access to the agenda of the day, being enacted. The students who were willing to take her on engaged with her as peers.

Issues of Voice and Positionality

Our second professor, Dorothy Berkson, also teaches English literature at Lewis and Clark College, where she is presently chair of the department and one of the prominent voices in the Gender Studies Program. One hallmark of her teaching was that she began class by having students read from their journals. Her purpose was to spark engagement, to get students to interact with the assigned texts and with one another, and to explore the positions that they had taken on the readings.

In her interview Berkson described her goals as "empowering students to think for themselves, to ask questions, to challenge virtually every-thing. . . . Of course I have the agenda of exposing them to feminist ideas. I think exposing them is probably the way I feel, not imposing it on them. It is a way of empowering them and I think it is a way for the male students to ask questions about power too."

The excerpts below are from a class on women writers taught in 1987, which included seventeen women and five men ranging from first-year students to seniors. At the previous class meeting, students had been struggling to interpret Emily Dickinson's poems. Berkson had ended that class by telling the students to go back and reread the poems and to do another journal entry based on what they had learned from the day's discussion. This current class began with her asking if anyone had taken her advice and tried to write about Emily Dickinson. Nancy, a very quiet Japanese American who often sat on the edge of the room, nodded and Berkson asked her to read what she had written. Nancy based her journal entry on the following Dickinson poem (all poetry citations from Johnson, 1967):

> I'm Nobody! Who are you?
> Are you—Nobody—Too?
> Then there's a pair of us?
> Don't tell! They'd advertise—
> you know!
> How dreary—to be—Somebody!
> How public—like a frog—
> To tell one's name—the live—
> long June
> to an admiring Bog!

Nancy's journal entry began as follows:

I couldn't help thinking of the idea of a mute culture within a dominant culture. A "nobody" knowing she's different from the dominant culture keeps silent and is surprised to find out there are others who share this feeling. But they speak only to each other and hide otherwise. This is what it must have been like being a woman and thinking against the grain. But don't tell! At least if you are silent and no one knows, you can continue to live your inner life as you wish, your thoughts at least still belong to you. If "they," the somebodies find out, they'll advertise and you'll have to become one of them.

But to be somebody! How dreary! How public! She says, "To tell one's name the livelong day to an admiring bog!" What is a name? I think she means an easily classifiable public identity. Names don't really tell you anything about what a person is like. So when you become a somebody and buy into the dominant culture, you have to live in their roles. You could call yourself a wife and the admiring bog says lovely, Yes. You could call yourself a spinster even and the bog would still admire you because you fit. But what if you don't want to be any of these things? Well then you stay a nobody. Nobodies, though silent and secretive at least have their peace, their solitude and are free from the judgment of the bog. (This could also be read about genius.)

Nancy was drawing here on what anthropologists Shirley and Edwin Ardener call "the wild zone." In Showalter's account of the Ardeners' conceptualization of culture, she states that women are a "muted group, the boundaries of whose culture and reality overlap but are not wholly contained by the dominant (male) group. Both muted and dominant groups generate beliefs or order ideas of social reality at the unconscious level but dominant groups control the forms or structures in which consciousness can be articulated" (Showalter, 1985, p. 29). Nancy also wrote some comments about the following Dickinson poem:

> Before I got my eye put out
> I liked as well to see—
> As other Creatures, that have
> Eyes
> And know no other way—
>
> But were it told to me—Today—
> That I might have the sky
> For mine—I tell you that my
> heart
> Would split, for size of me—

The Meadows—mine—
The Mountains—mine—
All Forests—Stintless Stars—

As much of Noon as I could
take
Between my finite eyes—

The Motions of the Dipping
Birds
The Morning's Amber Road—
for mine—to look at when I
liked—
The News would strike me dead—

So safer—guess—with must my
soul
Upon the Window pane—
Where other Creatures put their eyes—
Incautious—of the Sun

Nancy wrote the following comments about this poem:

[Dickinson] said: But let me try to go back to the inner and outer circles of society or rather back to the ideas of the dominant and mute cultures and the dangers and opposition that exists.

Those termed "mad" by the society, while more rewarded on a higher plane, still suffer here. You are either forced to conform and lose that sanity or you live under all sorts of social chains that keep you "still" and quiet, mute.

But looking at [the poem] it's problematic, there is a price to pay, and it isn't always voluntary. Infinite vision seems to come from suffering through enforced pain. "Before I got my eye put out/I liked as well to see—/As other Creatures, that have/Eyes/and know no other way." You can run around in ignorant bliss until something breaks through this level of illusion, take out the "eye" that makes it through it, you can't go back, trying to face yourself backwards would "strike you dead." I'm not articulating this well but it's like growing awareness.

A silly example: It's like watching a Walt Disney film as a child where Hayley Mills and these other girls dance and primp before a party singing "Femininity" how being a woman is all about looking pretty and smiling pretty and acting stupid to attract men. As a child I ate it up—at least it seemed benign, at the most I eagerly studied it. But once your eye gets put out and you realize how this vision has warped you, it would split your heart to try and believe that again, it would strike you dead. Much safer with your soul "upon the window pane."

Nancy's journal reading of the poem stopped the rest of the class dead. Berkson attempted to help the students engage with her ideas by asking Nancy to summarize, but the entry proved too complex for them. After a few of the students made unrelated comments, Berkson reviewed the concept of a mute culture within the dominant culture. She then tried again to draw students into a discussion of Nancy's ideas. When they did not respond, she turned to Nancy, as the authority, who then reiterated the meaning of what she had written. A discussion ensued between two students and Berkson, suggesting that Nancy's journal entry gave voice to all of them and revealed the ways that they thought about their relationship to the dominant culture.

SUSAN [a white student described as one of the class leaders]: That's because it's like a gift that puts you in the dominant cultural role and then you kind of owe it something, you can't just have it both ways. You can't believe in the subculture because you've got this gift, and if you want to keep it, you've got to stay somebody and that's got a price to pay.

BERKSON: This is really interesting. Anybody else?

MARCY [another Asian-American student]: When I read it, it was more like when she's a nobody, you know she's proud of being a nobody, she's a person, she's someone other than the majority. She had identified with that and she's kind of shocked when she finds that there is actually another person who doesn't want to be part of the majority also. When she says, "Oh how dreary to be somebody," its like oh how dreary to be part of the majority. You don't stand out, you just kind of like go in and mix with the majority. Whereas when you are a nobody you are someone.

BERKSON: Think about the person who doesn't want to be a member of the majority and who chooses to be a public flake, etcetera, but to be nobody is a different kind of choice, it is really to disappear from that public arena into the private sphere or the wild zone.

MARCY: You don't have to answer to anyone and you just can be yourself.

BERKSON: It's totally on your terms, it doesn't have to be on their terms at all.

MARCY: You are your own individual.

BERKSON: Yes.

NANCY: To add to that of what I thought is just to maintain that, to be able to maintain that, you had to be silent, you couldn't let anyone know, kind of. You have to be really sneaky.

BERKSON: To go back to Nancy's ideas about telling the truth "slant." It is like you don't want to give away too much of the truth in her terms. It can't be told straight out, there is a sense again that the usual structures somehow get slanted, get circumvented, get changed or altered or have to be gone around. The whole concept of the brightness that blinds is a power image for Dickinson.

Nancy's journal entries are a particularly powerful example of a previously silenced student coming to "voice." Nancy's imagery of "a nobody knowing she's different from the dominant culture," breaking through the illusion of "ignorant bliss," all combines to reveal this journal entry as a moment of awakening for her. She connected what she was learning—the Ardeners' concept of a mute culture within a dominant culture and Dickinson's poetry—with her experience as a woman, and perhaps as a minority woman. Nancy's identification with the positions of those who have been profoundly silenced was a perspective informed by and inseparable from her development as a knower and a learner. Her insights were subjective, not attempts at universal "truths."

In the conclusions of her journal entry, Nancy used powerful metaphors to depict her awakening. Her "silly example" implies that she was breaking through the illusion of a Japanese American patterning herself after Hayley Mills, a prototypical, blond teenager from the 1960s, and suggests that she was thinking of ethnicity as well as gender. However, while there are numerous references to gender in this journal entry, there is no explicit mention of race or ethnicity. When we first asked her if her journal entry related to her personal experience, she said that she did not "think about it in terms of an incident. Maybe an overlying personal experience. I really didn't think about that." But later in a follow-up interview, she said the following:

> There's no way that it could not, because obviously it had to connect to something and even I think the fact that when I put in about the example—I don't think there's a way you could be able to think about that sort of a concept of culture if you have not felt like you've lived it. . . . You know just even thinking in terms of race, even thinking about different kinds of minority perspectives, I guess, things like that I think I've started to look more into experience instead of just thinking about these theories. . . . I think that is something that sort of came out of this class. . . . I really have grown up in this community where everybody is blond and tall. . . . We are the only Japanese people, and since we never had really any Japanese community, I was never aware of that aspect in myself. Which doesn't mean that that didn't have any influence on the interactions, it just meant that I was not aware of that as influencing.

Thus, while her ethnic position had not been mentioned in the class discussion, Nancy later began to think about "looking more into" her ethnic experience as a result of Berkson's class. This novelty suggests how little Nancy's previous education had attended to issues of race or ethnicity.

We see this class session as particularly evocative of the themes of positionality and voice. Not only did Nancy speak from the explicit position of someone on the margins, but Berkson here *repositioned* her own relationship to the students and the students' relationship to the materials, beginning when the students, not Berkson, raised questions and set the agenda. The first voice to be taken seriously was a student's. By acknowledging Nancy's responses to Dickinson, her powerful connection to her own experience, Berkson let in the disruptive voices, the voices from the wild zone. Nancy's journal entry opened up new truths for other students, truths coming from different perspectives, thus exposing the shortcomings of any purportedly universalized, single truth.

The influence of Berkson's repositioning was observed in several other ways as well. First, while some students contributed frequently and consistently to classroom discussions, quieter students such as Nancy spoke more after they had read from their journals. Second, while female students learned to see their positions as women (and minorities) as generating newly valid knowledge about the world, male students became more conscious of power relations in the classroom and learned to listen. Duke, one of the five males in the class, spoke in his interview about the importance of hearing female voices. He was interested in finding out how "women feel about these texts": "I could read Dickinson a thousand times and probably never try to relate to that because it just would never make an impression on me, but having the girls in that class interested in that particular topic—'How does that relate to me as a woman?'—then I sit back and I think that's a really good question, and although I'm male I can sit and learn something from this and learn how women react to women's texts as opposed to maybe the way I react to it or Dorothy reacts to it or something like that." As Duke's comment shows, this empowering of females occasioned a fundamental change in the males' positions as well.

Nancy's journal entry also turned out to be a revelatory moment for Berkson. Although issues of race and ethnicity were implicit in Nancy's striking metaphorical connection to Hayley Mills, and in Berkson's comments, issues of race and ethnicity were not explicitly discussed that day. Berkson, however, recognized immediately that the students who had the most profound response to Dickinson's representation of a mute culture were the Japanese-American women. This led her, a few days after the Dickinson discovery, to share her thinking about the limitations of the syllabus with her students: "I told the class today, the thing that is really wrong with this course is that it is too Wasp, too Wasp, too British-American mainstream women writers, and I really need to think about that and how to change that. You know, I just don't think that the issues of race and gender and the way that different groups are disempowered or lose their voices can be really separated and those issues have been touched on in the course, but not enough. White women writers are overrepresented. I really want to do something about that."

Thus, through her reliance on student journals to determine the direction of class discussions, Berkson gave Nancy a chance to create and display a new reading of Emily Dickinson's poems, a reading from the explicit standpoint of a woman and the implicit standpoint of a Japanese American. The awakening of this student's voice produced changes in others' positions as well—the males' views were no longer at the center of the discourse and the teacher herself was inspired to change her syllabus. Moreover, this class was able to construct knowledge out of the intersection of new and partial truths, truths coming from the explicit identification of perspectives not heard before as "gendered" and "cultured" voices.

Conclusion

How can we summarize the ways that these two teachers constructed their alternative pedagogies? In the traditional classroom, to oversimplify things a bit, teachers' pedagogical choices are the guiding theories and worldview of a particular discipline. However, feminist theorists (and postmodernists) say that all worldviews are necessarily limited, that truth is partial. Depending on one's position, truth is gendered, raced, and classed. It is also dependent on context, including the context of the classroom, so that, for example, a woman's text and a feminist teacher may bring new truths forward while marginalizing others that used to occupy center stage.

If truth is partial, dependent on context, and yet, paradoxically, available to us through attention to particular positions and the lenses that they employ, then feminist teachers must be newly conscious of some aspects of teaching hidden from us by the traditional paradigms. One aspect is that we are particular (and evolving) knowers—the sources of our authority lie in our experience and our history, not centrally in our greater mastery of the abstract universals of our disciplines. A second aspect is that along with the illusion of perfect mastery, there is the illusion of the perfect teacher. In the literature on feminist pedagogy, for example, we constructed her as the consummate feminist, a teacher who is cooperative, compassionate yet demanding, and open-minded yet clear and resolute.

In the real situations of real classrooms, in the face of the need to make specific choices based on their own positions and the backgrounds and needs of their students, our two teachers took particular stands, at odds with traditional forms but also different from each other. While these two professors used student journals to start discussions, their choice of readings in their courses set the terms for the very different directions that they took. Dorothy Berkson, out of her commitment to women's awakening voices, used women's literature to consciously empower her students and evoke voices from the margins of traditional discourse, but she also allowed herself to evolve from a white woman's standpoint as a result of learning from minority women's experiences. Laurie Finke's literary theory course sought to get the theory clear, to come to a kind of definitive closure more usually associated with traditional models of teaching. And yet, on the day cited here, the theory itself was about partial truths, about gender and race and class as relational, positional, and changing in dynamic contexts. In creating this clarity, however, Finke seemed to ignore at one point the material condition of women as articulated by a persistent Jane.

As each teacher made her choices, she repositioned the relationships among herself, the students, and the material, away from herself as authority and toward learning as a function of complex interactions among teacher and student voices. These choices had different effects on different students, that is, different students learned different things. Nancy, awakened by Berkson and by Emily Dickinson, taught Duke, who was not used to a woman's perspective (or, we would guess, of thinking of himself as having a particular perspective). Finke energized Ned, Sam, and Jane through their give and take, but Carole felt both challenged and silenced in the same class.

So what questions do such teaching practices raise for issues of pedagogy in general? Our own meanings as teachers are evolving these days, as we attempt to listen to our students' questions and to keep up with the shifting grounds of gendered knowledge construction in our disciplines. Our student bodies are already over 50 percent female and are becoming increasingly ethnically diverse; this multiplicity of student backgrounds gives us a constantly expanding set of perspectives to contend with and honor as valid. Feminist approaches are not a panacea, or even a ready-made set of techniques. Rather, they are ways of dealing with difficult and recurrent choices between confusion and complexity, on the one hand, and clarity at the expense of some people's voices, on the other. The solutions nowadays are to be sought at the level of process, and in terms of the demands and goals of a particular teacher and classroom. Therefore, we believe that the most useful and evocative texts about feminist pedagogy are probably ethnographic in nature, detailing the specifics of teaching in different contexts. Finally, if the goals of gender integration are really to empower all our students, then we have to seek this empowerment not only at the level of course content but also at the level of our pedagogy. As teachers, we need to acknowledge our own development as a process, our own truths as partial, and yet affirm our own commitments and experiences as the only valid bases for our authority. Then we can respond to the multiple and interacting perspectives given by our students' voices and create new processes of knowledge construction beyond the traditional paradigms.

References

Alcoff, L. "Cultural Feminism Versus Post-Structuralism: The Identity Crisis in Feminist Theory." *Signs,* 1988, *13* (3), 405–436.

Belenky, M. F., Clinchy, B. M., Goldberger, N. R., and Tarule, J. M. *Women's Ways of Knowing: The Development of Self, Body, and Mind.* New York: Basic Books, 1986.

Haraway, D. "Situated Knowledges: The Science Question in Feminism and Privilege of Partial Perspective." *Feminist Studies,* 1988, *14* (3), 575–599.

Harding, S. *The Science Question in Feminism.* Ithaca, N.Y.: Cornell University Press, 1987.

Heath, S. B. *Ways With Words: Language, Life, and Work in Communities and Classrooms.* New York: Cambridge University Press, 1983.

Johnson, T. H. (ed.). *Complete Poems of Emily Dickinson.* New York: Macmillan, 1967.

Maher, F. "Classroom Pedagogy and the New Scholarship on Women." In M. Culley and C. Portuges (eds.), *Gendered Subjects: The Dynamics of Feminist Teaching.* London, England: Routledge & Kegan Paul, 1985a.

Maher, F. "Pedagogies for the Gender Balanced Classroom." *Journal of Thought,* 1985b, *20* (3), 48–64.

Moi, T. *Sexual/Textual Politics: Feminist Literary Theory.* London, England: Methuen, 1985.

Rich, A. "Claiming an Education." In *On Lies, Secrets and Silences: Selected Prose, 1966–1978.* New York: Norton, 1979.

Showalter, E. (ed.). "Feminist Criticism in the Wilderness." In *The New Feminist Criticism: Essays on Women, Literature, and Theory.* New York: Pantheon, 1985.

FRANCES MAHER is associate professor and chair of the Department of Education at Wheaton College, Norton, Massachusetts.

MARY KAY THOMPSON TETREAULT is professor and dean in the School of Human Development and Community Service at California State University, Fullerton.

Campuses nationwide are struggling to find effective and appropriate responses to diversity in the classroom, with many clinging to the traditional and naive assumption that the classroom is a value-neutral space.

Creating Multicultural Classrooms: An Experience-Derived Faculty Development Program

Betty Schmitz, S. Pamela Paul, James D. Greenberg

Why is it important to provide faculty members and teaching assistants (TAs) with knowledge and skills for teaching in a multicultural classroom? Because multicultural classrooms are made, not born. And if they are made right, there will be a difference between classrooms that are warm and inviting to students and those that—for many—seem cold and uninviting.

The classroom has traditionally, and often naively, been viewed as a value-free space, a neutral territory, in which all those who enter have an equal chance to participate and learn. Yet, as increasing numbers of students who are different from those traditionally served by mainstream higher education have entered the classroom, their retention rates have been lower than average and below what their aptitudes and abilities have indicated. Questions have thus arisen about differential levels of support and encouragement of students. Some of these questions rightly focus on the climate reflected in the classroom and whether all students perceive that climate as inclusive and respectful of diversity.

A multicultural classroom is much more than a collection of students who vary according to age, class, ethnicity, gender, national origin, race, religion, sexual orientation, or other such variables that may, like these, be visible or invisible. The critical ingredient is a supportive learning environment fostered by a teacher who appropriately recognizes and values different cultural styles and perspectives and effectively engages students in the learning process. It is this environment of multicultural valuation—not just the presence of students of different characteristics and backgrounds—

that makes a classroom multicultural and creates the potential for a fully effective learning climate.

This vision of the multicultural classroom informed discussions and training experiences with a wide variety of faculty members and TAs over the past three years at the University of Maryland at College Park. In 1988, the university funded a comprehensive program in which improvements of undergraduate women's education and of the classroom environment for all students were a central focus. This program became the impetus for the development of a university policy statement on classroom climate, training-of-trainers activities for campus leaders interested in improvement of classroom teaching, and campuswide faculty and TA development programs.

Each of us had a major role in implementing the Classroom Climate Project. In this chapter, we describe the assumptions, process, and key decision points that guided the development of our program. We also summarize program components and make suggestions about how they can be transposed to other settings.

Program Development

An essential starting point for program development is institutional commitment. The university's Statement on Classroom Climate (Appendix A), developed by a committee of faculty members and students, placed responsibility on faculty members to review their teaching behaviors, and those of the TAs that they supervise, for subtle behaviors that discourage student learning. This statement provided the leverage needed for initiation of development activities, but not the motivation for faculty members to participate. What kind of training program encourages faculty members and TAs to evaluate classroom climate and attempt to create an effective multicultural learning environment? In choosing a framework for faculty development, we had to establish a clear statement of beliefs that supported the goals of the program and the rationale for the changes that our training implied.

Decision Point 1: Articulating a Program Rationale. At the University of Maryland at College Park, the need for the program emerged from studies on campus climate for women, including surveys of classroom climate, and from concerns about low retention and graduation rates of African-American students. These data provided justification for serious attention to the issue of classroom environment and led the administration to fund a comprehensive program of faculty and TA development for teaching in a multicultural classroom.

To develop a program rationale, program leaders convened a committee of faculty members and graduate students with expertise in training and in climate issues. This group predicted that we could engage faculty members intellectually by asking them to think about complex questions such as the following: (1) What factors lead to differential educational outcomes for students of comparable skill and talent? (2) How do students learn in our classrooms and when does difference make a difference? (3) What are the implications for teaching and learning?

Some of the answers to these complex issues lie in the premise that teaching that includes and respects differences is likely to be more effective for learners and more satisfying for teachers. This kind of teaching draws on a wider array of potential resources, and it embraces all learners in the process. Thus, the rationale for the training program is rooted in the triple benefit of more effective pedagogy, greater likelihood of student retention, and enhancement of educational equity.

The committee also felt that programs that linked excellence in teaching with attention to diversity in the classroom would be the most effective. Resources such as the American Association for Higher Education's (1987) *Seven Principles of Good Practice for Undergraduate Education* serve as an excellent means of examining one's instructional techniques and determining areas for improvement. Principle 7, for example, is "Good Practice Respects Diverse Talents and Ways of Learning." A self-assessment on this item alone suggests that the creation of positive multicultural learning environments is an inherent part of good teaching.

Decision Point 2: Choosing a Theoretical Framework for Development Programs. The goal of faculty development programs in preparing teachers for the multicultural classroom is to provide them with an understanding of the impact of diversity on classroom dynamics so that they can make behavioral changes that improve the learning environment for all students. Consequently, learning and behavioral change theory provides a solid framework for the development of the training model.

Based on the learning cycle models developed by Kolb (1984), Kolb, Rubin, and McIntyre (1984), and by Jones, Pfeiffer, and Argyris, Palmer developed a useful framework for faculty development programs (Palmer, 1981). Palmer's model for learning and behavioral change includes four stages. The first stage, *discovering*, focuses on developing insight and gaining knowledge or understanding of the behavior of oneself and others. In the second stage, *formulating new behaviors*, individuals consider new behavioral alternatives with extensive discussion of their implications. The effectiveness of the third stage, *producing new behaviors*, is largely dependent on the level of motivation generated at the two previous stages. The fourth stage, *generalization to the real world*, is the final stage in this behavioral change process, in which individuals go back to their home setting and actually make changes in behavior based on learning. For the purposes of a faculty development program, these processes of change involve (1) awareness, (2) contemplation of change, (3) activities directed toward change, and (4) maintenance of change.

This approach, which might be called a cognitive behavioral model, differs from sensitivity training and prejudice-reduction models in that the focus is on specific behavioral change through a combination of cognitive and experiential activities with clear applicability to the classroom setting. The emphasis on intense emotional experiences and the here-and-now of some sensitivity awareness programs is not included in this model. Rather, this development program emphasizes an understanding of the impact of difference on behaviors and on problem solving in the classroom. Participants come to understand that cultural differences are part of our socialization process and that the resultant behaviors (for example, differential meaning accorded to eye contact between student and teacher) can impede student learning in the classroom.

Decision Point 3: The Content of the Development Program. Underlying this model and almost every other model of behavior change is the assumption that individual motivation to change is essential. Internal motivation can be greatly enhanced by external factors. Thus, knowledge about the changing demographics of the student body and society in general, real student experiences at the institution, and institutional values, policies, and programs related to multiculturalism are likely to establish the need for the development of teaching methods that effectively respond to increasing diversity on campus. Provision of faculty members and TAs with often startling data on differential patterns of student retention and graduation or with direct statements from students about classroom experiences can create a real desire to address these issues.

However, presentation of information about characteristics of specific groups (for example, older students, African Americans, women, and students with disabilities) cannot be accomplished effectively in one-to-three-hour time periods, the average amount of time available for initial programs directed to entire departmental faculties and TAs. The material is complex, and the potential for oversimplification and stereotyping of individuals based on group characteristics is too great. The content of our programs thus focuses on specific behaviors that encourage student learning, behaviors that should be avoided altogether, and behaviors that are applicable to all students.

The factors that affect interactions across groups include cultural values, perceptions, experiences (individual and group), communication styles, conflict styles, and assumptions. These factors become the focus of effective development efforts. Since all of these factors cannot be covered effectively in short time periods, development efforts should center on helping instructors to become better problem solvers and more sensitive to the significance of diverse cultural values and the ways in which they affect behaviors and perceptions in the classroom.

As emphasized in new learning theory, workshop design needs to take into consideration the cognitive dimensions of teaching and to recognize that teachers "build, through experience in contextualized situations, multiple scripts" that provide the basis for problem solving (Merseth, 1990).

Case studies or classroom scenarios are good ways to present for analysis recognizable problems in the classroom and assumptions and values that must be taken into account in order to solve these problems. Discussion of real classroom situations allows faculty members to identify problems and issues, their assumptions about the dimensions of these issues, and strategies to improve teaching (see sample classroom scenarios in Appendix B).

The expected outcome of these development programs is that faculty members become more effective with all students. This outcome results from the combined impact of an understanding of how cultural values shape decisions and behaviors, knowledge of the behaviors that discourage learning, motivation to make change, and information on specific behavioral changes that enhance the learning process (see program content in Appendix C and selected readings in Appendix D).

Decision Point 4: Deciding on a Pedagogical Approach and Testing the Model. In order to foster understanding of how to create an environment that responds to different learning styles, the development program should utilize as many different pedagogical strategies as possible. Some learning style preferences derive from cultural differences. For example, if a learning environment reflects a teaching-learning process characterized by individual and independent effort, competitive achievement measures, and time-dependent assessment, one cultural style is favored. However, if the environment emphasizes cooperative learning groups, shared effort, and assessment that is not time-dependent, other cultural styles may be favored. The use of diverse instructional strategies and methods of assessment in order to connect to the learning style preferences and differences among program participants reflects attention to multicultural needs. Some pedagogical strategies to include in programs are lecture, discussion, small group exercises, individual assessment tools, audiovisual aids, and reading material for preparation and follow-up.

Another important principle for program design and implementation is that modeling is a powerful form of learning. Training about diversity is more effective if the program leaders themselves demonstrate the effectiveness of diversity by working collaboratively in pairs that represent different genders and/or ethnicities. It is also essential for faculty members and TAs to serve as workshop leaders for peers and to use nonbiased language, inclusive examples, and appropriate humor.

We tested the effectiveness of the program in a two-stage training-of-trainers workshop with a diverse group of faculty, graduate students, and staff. The first stage was a focus group evaluation of the model, after which we made modifications. The second stage, a six-hour workshop, covered the entire range of the content and developed participants' skills as workshop leaders.

Decision Point 5: Formats and Scheduling. Provision of diverse formats allows the program to reach all faculty. Two regularly offered formats are included in our project: one-hour and three-hour sessions. A single workshop leader presents the one-hour information session. This session uses a lecture-discussion format and includes information about the growing diversity of the student body, faculty, and general public; principles of effective teaching in relation to diversity; classroom behaviors that interfere with student learning; and strategies for changing those behaviors. This session responds to the awareness and contemplation phases of the change process described earlier. A three-hour session, conducted by two leaders representing diversity, includes information, self assessment, audiovisual aids, and small group analysis of classroom scenarios. This session covers the processes of awareness, contemplation, and activities directed toward change.

One or two intensive programs can be offered each year to cover the entire change process, including maintenance of change. These sessions, offered for twelve to fifteen people, are a minimum of three days in length, with a fourth day of follow-up for maintenance of change four to six weeks after the initial session. Content includes values, learning styles, communication styles, conflict styles, perceptions, and assumptions that affect interactions across diverse groups.

Decision Point 6: Evaluating the Success of Programs. We faced several difficulties in deciding how to evaluate the effectiveness of the Classroom Climate Project. While the new information acquired by faculty and teaching assistants can be measured at the end of sessions, there is no guarantee that this knowledge will be applied in the classroom setting. In addition, measurement of change in classroom climate presents several difficulties, including concerns about intrusion in the teacher-student relationship and the apparent inequity of collecting data about faculty members who are attempting to make positive changes in their teaching but not collecting comparable data about peers who are not participating in the effort. Moreover, the prospects of outside evaluators going into classrooms to study changes in climate and teacher-student interactions would have been opposed by many whose support was essential to the project. Based on these constraints, we limited the evaluation procedures to the following activities:

1. During each phase of the project, we monitored the number of requests for workshops or presentations as well as the number and seniority level of faculty and academic administrators who attended.
2. We also monitored the number of requests for follow-up workshops by departmental liaisons as an indication of the effectiveness of the presentations made to them.
3. Participants evaluated the effectiveness of the presentation formats, presenters' skills, relevance of content, and information learned. In addition,

verbal statements by workshop participants about their increased awareness, insights, and planned behavioral changes were noted.
4. We evaluated the content of the training for the workshop leaders through a written evaluation form both at the pilot sessions and at the actual training session.
5. A focus group of workshop leaders evaluated the context, presentation styles, and resource materials.
6. Anecdotal and incidental reports of progress provided an intuitive sense that the classroom climate is improving.

One of the interesting findings was that persons who self-selected the workshop tended to find the learning experience more beneficial than those who were required to attend. While this finding is not surprising, it does point to one of the concerns experienced in the development of this project, namely, the problem of finding effective ways to motivate individuals who most need this information to participate in training. Two recommendations were made by departmental representatives in response to that concern: (1) link merit pay, tenure, and promotion of faculty to participation in these types of training and to the incorporation of the new learning into teaching approaches and curriculum and (2) use accountability measures to ensure that each department provides learning opportunities in which faculty members can participate.

Summary of Program Components

Key program components for faculty and TA development on multicultural issues in the classroom are as follows (see Appendix E):
Needs Assessment. The task of setting goals and objectives for the training programs must be done within the context of the campus culture and climate and must fit the specific needs of that campus. The climate of the campus, that is, the nature and extent of tensions and hostilities, if any, between and among groups, determines the best way to assess needs. For example, it is probably ill-advised to conduct a survey of different groups' perceptions of one another when intergroup tension is high. Surveys, while demonstrating need, also produce feelings of guilt. It also has been our experience that a department will agree to training only if there is specific information regarding classroom climate issues in that department. Student and faculty focus groups are a good way to get this kind of information, as is asking for a summary of records or complaints from the campus office that handles student grievances.

An efficient and effective form of assessment is the inclusion of questions related to classroom climate on standardized teaching evaluation forms for the campus or the department. It is advisable to begin training before adding this component to evaluations, since many of the behaviors that detract from multicultural inclusiveness are inadvertent and faculty members can correct them readily once they have identified them.

Program Support. No program will be successful without support from all sectors of the campus. The ideal level of support includes an institutional mission statement that emphasizes the creation of a multicultural campus community, financial resources to set up a permanent program for faculty and TA development (including resources for permanent staff), a faculty culture that values professional development and teaching improvement and endorses the need for a positive multicultural environment, and student support for improved intergroup interactions on campus and in the classroom. Few institutions currently have this level of support, but programs can be built from a baseline of expertise and resources such as those described in this chapter.

One particularly effective strategy to garner support is to designate one senior faculty member per department to serve as the liaison with the project office. This person participates in an orientation meeting and becomes familiar with development programs and print and video resources to recommend to faculty and TAs in the department.

Resource Development. The development of resources includes selection and acquisition of materials, curriculum development, and training of personnel. Program directors or coordinators will find that there is a sizable body of literature available that deals with student diversity in the classroom. A major challenge in using this material is that it emanates from different fields—curriculum and instruction, multicultural education, women's studies, ethnic studies, and psychology, to name but a few—each field not only reflecting its own biases but also operating with assumptions and perspectives different from those of other fields. For example, most of the classroom climate literature has focused on gender, while the multicultural education literature has emphasized racial and ethnic diversity. It is essential to develop an inclusive and broad-based curriculum for the program in order to avoid fragmentation of issues and to reflect the range of pertinent conceptions in the area of classroom inclusiveness.

People who can serve as effective trainers are another essential component. Institutions are well served by investing in training-of-trainers programs (rather than relying on outside consultants) to produce a core of people to work with faculty members and TAs. The more diversity within this group, the more potential there is for producing inclusive curricula and effectively pairing workshop leaders for different campus audiences. The experience of these leaders within the campus community and the commitment that they demonstrate to the program make it harder for program participants to discount the training.

Faculty/TA Development. Development activities include workshops of varying length, classroom observation, readings and video materials, and self-assessment instruments. These services can be provided through existing offices, such as a center for teaching improvement or a human relations office, or through the creation of a new network of individuals who serve as project leaders. An important aspect of the program is the development of expertise in local units, especially on large campuses.

Evaluation. It is important to be explicit about the evaluation plan in relation to program goals: What is to be evaluated, for what purposes, and how? Evaluation can be used to inform both individual faculty members about teaching improvement and program leaders about modifications necessary to the program.

The essential feature of the evaluation process, however, is that it involve many individuals on campus. Students do evaluation of the program and of individual faculty members, who in turn evaluate program activities and provide input to the administration on both program and policy. Department chairs and senior administrators use evaluation data, including anecdotal data, to make decisions about program modification and resource allocation. This involvement of the entire campus community in the program ensures that it will continue to be rooted within the institutional context and be effective in meeting institutional goals for change.

References

American Association for Higher Education. *Seven Principles of Good Practice for Undergraduate Education—Faculty Inventory*. Racine, Wis.: Johnson Foundation, 1987.

Kolb, D. A. *Experiential Learning: Experience as the Source of Learning and Development*. Englewood Cliffs, N.J.: Prentice Hall, 1984.

Kolb, D. A., Rubin, I. M., and McIntyre, J. M. *Organizational Psychology: An Experiential Approach to Organizational Behavior*. Englewood Cliffs, N.J.: Prentice Hall, 1984.

Merseth, K. "Case Studies and Teacher Education." *Teacher Education Quarterly*, 1990, 17 (1), 53–72.

Palmer, A. B. "Learning Cycles: Models of Behavior Change." In J. E. Jones and J. W. Pfeiffer (eds.), *The 1981 Annual Handbook for Group Facilitators*. San Diego, Calif.: University Associates, 1981.

Appendix A: The University of Maryland at College Park Statement on Classroom Climate

The University of Maryland at College Park values the diversity of its student body and is committed to providing an equitable classroom atmosphere that encourages the participation of all students. Patterns of interaction in the classroom between the faculty member and students and among the students themselves may inadvertently communicate preconceptions about student abilities based on age, disability, ethnicity, gender, national origin, race, religion, or sexual orientation. These patterns are due in part to the differences the students themselves bring to the classroom.

Classroom instructors should be particularly sensitive to being equitable in the opportunities they provide students to answer questions in class, to contribute their own ideas, and to participate fully in projects in and outside of the classroom.

Of equal importance to equity in the classroom is the need to attend to potential devaluation of students that can occur by reference to demeaning stereotypes of any group and/or overlooking the contributions of a particular group to the topic under discussion. Joking at the expense of any group creates an inhospitable environment and is inappropriate. Moreover, in providing evaluations of students, it is essential that instructors avoid distorting these evaluations with preconceived expectations about the intellectual capacities of any group.

It is the responsibility of individual faculty members to review their classroom behaviors, and those of any teaching assistants they supervise, to ensure that students are treated equitably and not discouraged or devalued based on their differences. Resources for self-evaluation and training for faculty members on classroom climate and interaction patterns are available from the Office of Human Relations.

Appendix B: Sample Classroom Scenarios

Discuss the issues involved in the following teaching situations and how you would resolve them. Provide a solution from the teacher's and the student's points of view.

1. Dr. Newly Hired is concerned that the male students dominate class discussions in her twenty-person senior philosophy seminar. The men readily speak up and often continue to pursue their points in heated debate with one another and with her. The women students, on the whole, are more reticent and less willing to continue to debate a point either with her or with their male peers. The women students are interrupted frequently, and their ideas not acknowledged by other students. There are fourteen male and six female students in the course.

2. One of your friends, who teaches the introductory survey of art history, has just learned that a student who is blind has enrolled in the class. The friend asks you for ideas on how to teach this student. The classroom work almost entirely involves analysis of slides of the art, and your friend, while concerned about access for students with disabilities, doesn't see how accommodation is possible.

3. For the past month, Dr. Mary Land has noticed that all seven African-American students sit in the back of her fifty-person class. Their grades are lower than those of the white students; however, their attendance is above average. They seldom participate in class discussions, upon which a portion of the grade is based.

4. Dr. Hugh Moore frequently uses jokes and sarcasm to spice up his

lectures. In class one day, a woman student challenges his lecturing technique because he always uses terms like "he" and "man" that exclude women. "My dear," he responds, "man embraces woman." The class laughs at his witty response.

Appendix C: Content of Faculty Development Programs (One-Hour and Three-Hour Formats)

Topic 1: Demographic Data
Subtopics: changing student body, changing faculty, changing society
Purpose: to establish need for faculty to consider changing their classroom behaviors

Topic 2: Principles of Effective Teaching
Subtopics: student-faculty contact, cooperation among students, active learning, prompt feedback, time on task, high expectations of all students, respect for diverse talents and learning styles
Purpose: to establish joint assumptions about what constitutes effective teaching

Topic 3: Differences in the Classroom
Subtopics: impact of age, culture, class, disability, ethnicity, gender, national origin, race, religion, and sexual orientation of faculty and students on classroom dynamics
Purpose: to encourage faculty members to acknowledge the difference that difference makes in the classroom setting

Topic 4: Classroom Behaviors That Can Discourage Learning
Subtopics: ignoring students, cultural differences in eye contact, expectations, singling out differences, joking, put-downs, interruptions, overprotectiveness, condescension, stereotyping, communication styles, learning styles
Purpose: to create a relationship between faculty behavior and student learning; in each category, to discuss and give examples of both effective and noneffective behaviors in order to replace negative behaviors with positive ones

Topic 5: Effects of Negative Classroom Behaviors on Learning
Subtopics: discourages participation, discourages help seeking, encourages dropouts, lowers confidence, lowers expectations, inhibits faculty-student communication, inhibits creativity
Purpose: to develop positive relationships between faculty behaviors and effects on students

Topic 6: Evaluation of the Need for Change
Subtopics: peer evaluation of classroom behaviors, student evaluations of classroom behaviors, videotaping classrooms, self-evaluation checklists

Purpose: to help faculty identify specific areas of behavior on which they might focus

Topic 7: Specific Strategies for Change

Subtopics: clearly stated expectations, open communication with students, developing awareness and checklists for noticing, experiment with different assignments, seating arrangements, ways of recognizing students, ways of asking questions, different questions, noticing humor, evaluation of curriculum materials for omission and bias, monitor student-student interactions, observing nonverbal messages

Purpose: to provide tools for modifying behaviors once areas in need of change have been identified

Topic 8: Resource Packages

Subtopics: follow-up readings (two to five articles), list of people to contact for further assistance, selected bibliography, list of follow-up workshops, checklists

Purpose: to provide follow-up resources for those who wish to learn more about specific groups

Appendix D: Selected Readings for Follow-up Workshops

Bagasao, P. Y. "Student Voices: Breaking the Silence—The Asian and Pacific American Experience." *Change,* Nov.-Dec. 1989, pp. 28-37.

Collins, P. H. "Getting Off to a Good Start: The First Class in Black Family Studies." *Teaching Sociology,* 1986, *14,* 193-195.

Commission on Minority Participation in Education and Life. *One-Third of a Nation.* Washington, D.C.: American Council on Education, 1988.

Greene, M. F. (ed.). *Minorities on Campus: A Handbook for Enhancing Diversity.* Washington, D.C.: American Council on Education, 1989.

Hall, R. M., and Sandler, B. R. *The Classroom Climate: A Chilly One for Women?* Washington, D.C.: Project on the Status and Education of Women, Association of American Colleges, 1982.

Jenkins, M. M. *Removing Bias: Guidelines for Student-Faculty Communication.* Annandale, Va.: Speech Communication Association, 1983.

Thorne, B. "Rethinking the Ways We Teach." In C. S. Pearson, D. L. Shavlick, and J. G. Touchton (eds.), *Educating the Majority: Women Challenge Tradition in Higher Education.* New York: American Council on Education/ Macmillan, 1989.

Appendix E: Classroom Climate Project Program Components

Area 1: Needs Assessment

Means of implementation: teaching evaluations, surveys of classroom climate, faculty-student focus groups, reports

Persons responsible: department chairs, administrators, faculty members
Outcome: demonstrates that problem exists and in what forms

Area 2: Support from Faculty, Administrators, and Students
Means of implementation: policy statement adopted, statement approved, funds provided, responsibilities designated, committees formed
Persons responsible: faculty governing body, senior administrators, student government
Outcome: consensus built around need for change, formal policy platform

Area 3: Resource Development
Means of implementation: training model, training of trainers, checklists, readings
Persons responsible: program director, campus experts, consultants
Outcome: center of responsibility created, resources in place

Area 4: Faculty/TA Development
Means of implementation: training, observation, resource provision
Persons responsible: trainers and experts, resource office staff
Outcome: skilled and knowledgeable teachers, local unit enhancement, changes in priorities

Area 5: Evaluation
Means of implementation: evaluation of training, survey of classroom climate, teaching evaluations
Persons responsible: program director, department chairs
Outcome: program modifications, teaching modifications

BETTY SCHMITZ is senior associate, Office of Women in Higher Education, American Council on Education.

S. PAMELA PAUL is director of multicultural affairs, Loyola College, Baltimore, Maryland.

JAMES D. GREENBERG is project coordinator for the Center for Teaching Excellence, University of Maryland at College Park.

This chapter presents a survey of eight universities' programs for helping faculty and teaching assistants meet the instructional needs brought about by changing campus populations.

Improving the Climate: Eight Universities Meet the Challenges of Diversity

Diane R. vom Saal, Debrah J. Jefferson, Minion KC Morrison

As a nation, we are moving into a new phase in our history. The diversity that has always been interwoven in the fabric of our culture is predicted to increase in the workplace and in educational settings in unprecedented proportions. Are universities ready to deal with this challenge? Yes and no. Although there is much need for research on multicultural teaching and learning, the eight universities highlighted in this chapter are attempting to meet the instructional needs of a changing campus population. They are at different stages in their answers to the challenge of diversity, their programs reflect their own campus cultures and values, and their programs for fostering diversity in the instructional and classroom environment are housed in various locations. Yet, certain trends emerge from descriptions of their programs.

Each institution has made conscious choices about target groups to be covered in sessions designed to increase sensitivity. Most programs emphasize racism and sexism, but issues of other target groups also are addressed, for example, homophobia, xenophobia, heterosexism, ableism, ageism, anti-Semitism, and classism. All sources interviewed expressed a desire for more information on the instructional needs of target groups as well as on ways to increase sensitivity in academic settings.

Program planners are aware of media accusations of unfair pressure for "political correctness" on college campuses. Most planners are working to ensure that participants at workshops and seminars understand the difference between pressure for political correctness and sensitivity training to promote a positive climate for all campus community members. There is also a common belief in the benefits of diversity in terms of the enrichment of campus intellectual life. Program planners are aware that the issue of diversity has brought much needed attention to the importance of student-centered teaching and have incorporated the enhancement of teaching in general into goals for diversity training.

The role of the administrator is important in supporting activities to meet the challenges and opportunities of our rapidly changing campuses. Insights into administrators' functions are covered here after the program descriptions. These descriptions touch on goals, organizational designs, and future plans for selected instructional programs at eight universities.

University of Colorado, Boulder

Administrators at the University of Colorado support multicultural concerns from the top: The president has made multiculturalism a part of the strategic plan and has set up the Fund for the Retention of Women and Minorities; the Boulder campus chancellor established a Chancellor's Advisory Committee on Minority Affairs to advise him on campus policies and practices related to minority faculty, staff, and students; the vice chancellor for faculty affairs has developed programs to assist plurality faculty; the Faculty Teaching Excellence Program has held a yearly conference on women's issues in teaching and has plans to develop workshops on multicultural issues in teaching; and the graduate school has instituted programs to recruit and retain minority graduate students, while at the same time providing teaching assistants (TAs) with a multicultural development program administered through the regular campuswide TA training program, the Graduate Teacher Program (GTP).

GTP sessions on gender, race, and ethnicity are led by staff from several other campus groups who are trained to facilitate workshops: the Multicultural Center for Counseling and Community Development provides multicultural teams of black, Asian, Native American, Hispanic, and feminist therapists; the Center for the Study of Ethnicity and Race in America contributes full and associate professors to the pool of trained facilitators; and faculty from sociology, history, philosophy, education, linguistics, and women's studies who have done research related to gender, race, or ethnicity have also presented workshops. Other sessions on multicultural issues in the classroom have been led by staff from the University Learning Center, a minority undergraduate support unit, and the Office of Services for Disabled Students, whose learning disabilities staff provides at least one workshop per year. Interest in and attendance at workshops on gender and multicultural issues have been high; for example, ninety-five graduate teachers attended a two-day conference on issues of gender, race, and ethnicity in January 1991. In the past seven years more than seven hundred graduate teachers have voluntarily participated in multicultural workshops.

The GTP philosophy holds that all students should expect and receive equal access to education and equal classroom treatment from the instructor. Because the primary audience is graduate teachers, departmental cooperation is essential. Departments are encouraged to recommend attendance at the training sessions, which provide concepts that encourage bias-free teaching behaviors, ideas on including multicultural issues in the curriculum, ways to identify bias in assessment and evaluation, and ways to increase instructors' self-understanding. In 1990–1991, fourteen workshops were devoted to topics related to the "isms"—sexism, heterosexism, racism, ethnocentrism, ageism, classism, and ableism—and the schisms, homophobia and xenophobia. One workshop involves confronting sexual harassment issues through a theatrical presentation. When this workshop was presented at a recent national conference, an experienced participant stated that it was "by far the most powerful experience I've ever had on this issue."

The GTP staff consists of the director (86 percent time), three graduate assistants, and two undergraduate assistants. The program works from a strong theoretical and research base grounded in both gender studies and studies of race and ethnicity. A strong point of the program is the faculty and counselor involvement: forty-eight faculty and staff have assisted with multicultural training over the past seven years. Also helping to make the Colorado program strong is an evaluation process for program improvement based on participants' feedback. Participants attending at least four workshops are sent follow-up evaluation forms to measure the long-term effects of their training. Feedback is used to develop workshop or conference topics. The next stage is more networking and working with TA supervisors. (For more information, contact Laura Border, Graduate Teacher Program.)

Harvard University

Harvard has an "infusion model" to address issues of diversity. In this model, diversity activities are dispersed throughout the campus within existing structures. This approach has evolved over a number of years. The Derek Bok Center for Teaching and Learning (formerly the Danforth Center) is the locus of many activities related to the improvement of teaching; the task of directing attention to issues of diversity has become a part of these activities. The overall goal is to promote a positive climate and an inclusive spirit for all students.

The Bok Center coordinates large orientation sessions at the beginning of each semester for new faculty and teaching fellows. One theme of these sessions is "Teaching to Student Diversity." Along with workshops, the Harvard approach includes print and video materials. The Bok Center has recently finished producing a videotape, *Race in the Classroom: The Multiplicity of Experience,* for use in diversity workshops for students, faculty, and teaching fellows. The videotape includes five vignettes of incidents involving racial issues. The center also addresses gender issues in a new brochure for faculty and teaching fellows, and there are plans to create a similar flyer concerning racial issues. A handbook for teaching fellows and a guide for international faculty and TAs include information on teaching a diverse population of students. In 1992 the center plans a day-long conference on race and gender in the classroom similar to a gender conference of two years ago.

Activities also take place in individual graduate schools, such as the School of Public Health, which includes a case study with racial overtones in their sessions focusing on teaching. Another strategy in the School of Public Health is to ask faculty to fill out a questionnaire that invites them to think about how they handle issues involving diversity in the classroom.

Other groups also contribute to diversity training. The Office of Race Relations and Minority Affairs provides a link to undergraduate houses (residence halls) through designated "race-relations tutors" and offers further training through students who conduct workshops on difficulties such as racism and ethnocentrism throughout the year as well as during a designated week of awareness activities. Another organization, The Harvard Foundation, sponsors presentations by leaders of various minority communities. Issues important to students with disabilities are addressed by a student association called ABLE, in conjunction with the Office of Disability Resources and the Bok Center.

The Bok Center will continue its strategy of working within the existing campus culture by weaving issues of diversity into the present general training programs. The approach involves careful work with many people contributing to the final product. The intent is to foster a gradual strengthening of the communication and teaching skills that faculty and teaching fellows bring to the increasingly diverse student population. (For more information, contact Ellen Sarkisian, Derek Bok Center for Teaching and Learning.)

University of Hawaii

The University of Hawaii is addressing the diversity challenge because of a unique blend in its institutional community. While there is no ethnic majority, most students are Hawaiian, Asian, or Filipino, and most new faculty are U.S. mainland Caucasians. The university's Office of Faculty Development and Academic Support (OFDAS) has established the Center for Studies of Multicultural Higher Education (CeSOMHE) to address this issue through institutional research and campus outreach programs. The center is a research component of OFDAS but works with the Center for Teaching Excellence, also under OFDAS, to foster inquiry into issues of multicultural teaching and learning. CeSOMHE was established to work with faculty to advance scholarship applied to the study of teaching practice and the implications of cultural variables for student learning. The center's philosophy is that the cultures of both the student and the faculty member influence the teaching-learning process. Its goal is to generate and transmit information about multiculturalism applied to the teaching-learning process. The program's funding is integrated with other projects under OFDAS and also generates external funding for special projects.

Although training activities are secondary to CeSOMHE's research goal, their staff join with the Center for Teaching Excellence to apply research findings during several sessions for new faculty and TAs. CeSOMHE also disseminates its findings at roundtables to which faculty are invited. The focus is on racism, gender issues, and culture, particularly as related to Hawaii's ethnic groups. CeSOMHE has two full-time faculty members whose research areas are directly related to issues of multiculturalism. They work with forty-two faculty facilitators who also have expertise in this area.

CeSOMHE's strong point is its focus on research in an area with limited data. The setup is convenient because the Center for Teaching Excellence is ready to disseminate findings as CeSOMHE continues to look at campus issues of race and gender from sociological and anthropological viewpoints. One drawback is the time it takes to study these complex issues. Also, it is easy to take multiculturalism for granted on a campus with such a diverse population, and it is a challenge to keep the issue fresh and interesting.

Future plans include producing a training manual, publishing research, and applying findings in videotape presentations. An internal funding program, the Educational Improvement Fund, has made multiculturalism its theme for 1991 and 1992. CeSOMHE will continue conducting research and working on the applied stage of current research projects. (For more information, contact Marie Wunsch, Office of Faculty Development and Academic Support.)

University of Michigan, Ann Arbor

Academic and nonacademic units throughout the University of Michigan campus are involved in numerous programs that are designed to advance diversity issues and the development of a more multicultural approach in the curricula and in teaching. Recently, the Office of Minority Affairs sponsored an all-day Diversity Fair with booths and workshops by those on campus who have programs on diversity. Everyone attending the fair received a Diversity Directory, providing a comprehensive listing and brief description of past and present campus activities addressing multicultural issues.

There are numerous units on campus that are concerned with multicultural curriculum and pedagogy. The Center for Research on Learning and

Teaching (CRLT) has programs for both faculty and TAs that are designed to help them develop a more multicultural approach to their teaching and to engender an awareness of diversity issues in the classroom. A number of departments offer courses that address multicultural issues. The Faculty Against Institutional Racism Teaching Group is working, through a support network and workshops, to improve teaching in this area. The Intergroup Relations and Conflict Program has developed a series of new courses and minicourses in the area of conflict resolution. Various units with TA training programs include instruction that encourages and instructs TAs in the development of a multicultural approach to their teaching and sensitivity to diversity issues (CRLT, the College of Literature, Science, and Arts TA Training Program, and several departmental programs).

CRLT was founded almost twenty-five years ago with a mission to serve the entire campus. CRLT has for several years sponsored a variety of programs that are designed to enhance teaching and learning in a culturally diverse classroom environment. Workshops and training programs help instructors develop a more inclusive approach to their teaching through the use of techniques that address the diverse learning styles and levels of their students. The programs also assist instructors in creating a climate that is conducive to the growth and development of every student in their classes. Over the past two years, staff at the center have added several segments to workshops designed to help instructors become more aware of discrimination and its impact in the classroom. During the past year, CRLT added specific workshops called "multicultural teaching" for both faculty and TAs. However, issues addressed in such sessions are also infused throughout most CRLT workshops and training programs. (For more information, contact Beverly Black, Center for Research on Learning and Teaching.)

University of Missouri, Columbia

The University of Missouri's multicultural sensitivity program for faculty and TAs operates from the Program for Excellence in Teaching (PET). Two task forces are also making recommendations about future activities for faculty, staff, and students. The Task Force on Ethnic Civility, formed by the Faculty Council, and the Task Force on Gender Sensitivity Training, initiated by the provost, examine the present climate for all women, men of color, and other target groups. The gender sensitivity task force has created a protocol statement. PET and the task forces report to the Office of the Vice Provost for Minority Affairs and Faculty Development and coordinate their efforts. Funding for PET's diversity programming comes from its general operating funds. PET's program leaders have done doctoral work in communications and intergroup interaction.

PET staff believe that teaching and learning take place in a cultural context that is influenced by the background experience of the participants, and that all members of the university community have the right to feel welcome and safe. PET's workshops and seminars on diversity are designed to foster an understanding of intergroup communication and its influence on the campus climate and to emphasize awareness, empowerment, and action through interactive activities. New faculty and new TAs work on these issues during their orientations at the beginning of the fall semester. Sessions tailored for specific departments or units are presented by invitation during each semester. Individual faculty also request private consultation and resource materials on classroom climate. Recently, PET staff worked closely with the Multicultural Development Committee in the School of Journalism to offer six workshops on multiculturalism to faculty and professional staff. Another teaching improvement program, a faculty group called Wakonse, routinely addresses gender and race during informal discussions on teaching. A planning committee works with PET to hold campuswide teaching conferences, including sessions on multicultural issues.

In preparation for workshops and seminars, PET systematically gathers information to design workshops. PET staff gather information from informal interviews with departmental liaisons or through formal questionnaires addressed to all staff and faculty in a specific department or college. Formal written feedback from faculty and TAs at the end of workshops is used to revise workshops and to formulate follow-up plans. So far, the claim that attention to multicultural sensitivity is pressure for "political correctness" has not been an issue at the university. Still, PET staff believe that the program should be held accountable for promoting a positive climate for all campus community members.

The most important strength is the campus support from faculty, administrators, and students. In postworkshop comments, a faculty member wrote, "Continue the process. Don't let the flame burn out. This is just a start and we're finally taking some action. Some people seem shocked that case studies actually occur." Another strong point is that PET reports to the campus administrator who is responsible for both minority affairs and faculty development. Under these auspices, PET works closely with the Personnel Services/Affirmative Action Office and the Office of Academic Assistance to plan strategies for reaching all campus faculty, staff, and students. Students also have taken a strong stand on these issues and have independently formed a group called Students Organized Against Racism.

PET's program has taken the first step and is getting ready for the next stage. A full-time facilitator with separate funding is needed to continue the progress because of the size of the campus. To help reach more faculty, plans call for training a cadre of faculty and staff volunteers to join PET in presenting seminars and workshops. Work is also underway to develop and offer follow-up sessions that go beyond the awareness level of initial workshops. Research on human relations in classroom settings is also planned. (For more information, contact Diane R. vom Saal or Debrah J. Jefferson, Program for Excellence in Teaching.)

The Ohio State University

In 1987, The Ohio State University produced an action plan for the recruitment and retention of black faculty and students. As part of this plan, the Center for Teaching Excellence (CTE) was asked to develop seminars for faculty and TAs to sensitize them to the teaching needs of black students. Staff members in CTE's Faculty and Teaching Associate Development Program began studying the stages of racial awareness and deciding on realistic goals. They decided that awareness of one's own biases is the first step, followed by behavioral change and, finally, attitudinal change. CTE, which reports to the provost, was allocated funding from the central administration to carry out the program and is now expanding the program to include other special populations.

The planners consider diversity a strength and a hallmark of academic institutions. They also believe that the effort to improve the climate for black students on campus begins with the president, whose support is coupled with that of the provost, deans and other administrators, department chairs, and faculty and teaching associates. The main activity of the program was an individual departmental seminar presented by CTE staff and facilitators. These department seminars have reached most of the approximately 150 academic units on campus. Each seminar was presented by a team of two facilitators, one white and one black. Each was tailored to the specific department through planning with a departmental representative who cofacilitated the seminar. In some departments, faculty were addressed separately from teaching associates, and, in others, they met together, depending on the preference of the department. CTE designated a target group of colleges for seminars each quarter, usually five colleges per quarter. As many as five or six departmental seminars were given each week.

The design of the 1990–1991 seminars was based on research on retention data on black students and on work with current black students in the production of a videotape that tells their story. To begin the process leading to each seminar's presentation, the videotape was shown to each college's dean. The dean then joined the CTE director in writing a letter to each department to request that the seminar be held during a regular departmental meeting. Faculty and TAs were expected to attend. Seminar facilitators included seven CTE staff members and about thirty volunteers who were trained at two-day retreats held each quarter for new volunteers. Usually, the seminar consisted of five main components: (1) a summary of data on the retention of black students at Ohio State, (2) the videotape, (3) thoughts contributed by the departmental representative on the particular issues relevant to the department concerning black student retention, (4) a case study analysis or open-ended discussion of a personal assessment instrument, and (5) distribution of materials for effective teaching in the multicultural classroom.

Participants evaluated the seminar by filling out a form at the seminar's conclusion. Then, after two quarters, CTE asked a sample of participants for information on the long-term effects of the seminar. Future plans for the program are to expand topic coverage to sexism and homophobia as well as to special target groups, such as underprepared and high-risk students, students with physical and learning disabilities, and other ethnic groups. Plans are underway to prepare a group of faculty and teaching associates to become facilitators and trainers for this next phase. New faculty and TAs will participate in the program at their orientations. The department setting will continue to be used for experienced instructors. To have an informed and current program, CTE staff members look forward to conducting and using more research on the teaching and learning needs of minority students. (For more information, contact Nancy Van Note Chism, Center for Teaching Excellence.)

Stanford University

In order to finance a program to train TAs in multicultural issues, the Center for Teaching and Learning at Stanford successfully sought grant monies from a special fund that the Irvine Foundation had given the university. An ad hoc advisory board was then formed from diverse campus groups, along with one faculty member from each of the four departments that the program would initially target. This board helped the center, which reports to the vice president for student resources, plan the first phase of the program in 1990. The objective was to work initially with TAs, teaching fellows, and lecturers in those departments that teach required or popular introductory classes to freshmen. The graduate dean was also very supportive of this effort.

The program's philosophy stems from literature on forms of oppression. The goal of the program is to work toward better teaching for all by providing TAs with direct experience in multicultural issues. In its pilot phase, the program's activity was a sequence of two four-hour workshops conducted by a senior-level graduate student whose research area of modern thought and literature is directly related to multiculturalism. He, in turn, recruited other graduate students as cofacilitators. Both the graduate dean and the center's director made remarks during the workshops, which were held at the beginning of the year. TAs who participated were paid $50. The workshops were designed to be experiential so TAs could examine their own positions on multicultural issues rather than approach the topic from a purely academic viewpoint. The workshops covered issues relating to all target groups, with an emphasis on racism. Routine evaluation after each workshop has provided positive feedback and ideas for the design of future workshops. The current plans calls for expansion of multicultural training to all TAs by incorporating the material from the experimental first workshop into the annual general TA orientation, which will be expanded from a half day to a full day.

Program strengths include the support of the dean of graduate studies and of department chairs who encourage their TAs to attend the workshops. The funding from the Irvine Foundation grant has been a tremendous help. The high level of preparedness and commitment by the graduate student conducting the workshops also has been a strength. One frustration has been the challenge of helping TAs avoid the temptation to "intellectualize" about the issues. Another frustration has been the confusion and misinformation generated by the concept of political correctness. This program emphasizes that multiculturalism is not about having a "correct" line on how to deal with people but rather having an approach that will make learning more effective for all students.

Future plans of the center include cosponsorship of a seminar for faculty who not only will discuss multicultural issues but also will design a forum for outreach to their colleagues. Eventually, TAs and faculty across all departments will be touched by one or more of these efforts. (For more information, contact Michele Marincovich, Center for Teaching and Learning.)

University of Tennessee, Knoxville

To address concerns about diversity on campus, the program "Toward Equal Opportunity and Retention: A Change Model Using Video as a Strategic Change Agent" began in 1988 with a $90,000, three-year grant from the Fund for the Improvement of Post-Secondary Education. This program, emanating from the chancellor's office, was designed to improve race relations on the campus by helping faculty overcome negative feelings, attitudes, and behaviors affecting their interaction with students and by empowering faculty in their use of positive attitudes to affect the teaching and learning environment.

Faculty volunteer to attend eight to ten weekly sessions for four hours per week. One trainer leads discussion groups of eight to ten people in a guided exercise in which participants discover and change negative attitudes and beliefs in the supportive company of peers who reinforce each other's positive beliefs. In the process of discovery and discussion, various "isms" are confronted. Six videos—five simulating classroom experiences of black students with white faculty and one depicting a black faculty member going through the tenure process—have been produced for group discussion. Research materials and personal experiences enhance the process.

Although several types of evaluation have been used to measure the effectiveness of the project, the project codirector states, "The participants themselves are the greatest measure of the success of the project in their ability to look at themselves and their desire to want to do some things differently in the process." The project has received national attention, with a positive reception from other educators.

One of the strong points of the program is the length of time allowed for participants to deal with diversity issues in an environment free from repercussions. But time is also a source of frustration because faculty schedules may prevent them from attending some sessions. After the eight- to ten-week sessions are over, groups continue meeting monthly for lunch to share concerns and ideas.

Plans call for the establishment of a training institute to instruct future leaders interested in the application and institutionalization of the program. Other plans include the development of potential leaders from the faculty who attend the sessions. (For more information, contact Camille Hazeur, Office of Affirmative Action, or Dhyana Ziegler, Department of Broadcasting.)

Administrative Support for Multicultural Programs

The preceding program descriptions demonstrate why the contemporary administrator must be attuned to the needs of a vastly changed university in the United States. These descriptions reveal a common thread in the institutions surveyed: The university must deal with a plethora of new clients, many of whom arrive at an academy that historically has denied them full access. This condition has led institutions to devise strategies and means not merely for broadening representation but also for improving the quality of the environment in academic programs in light of the new inclusiveness. Thus, many faculty development centers have engaged in this process by training faculty and others to enhance their teaching in a diverse, multicultural, contemporary university.

Frequently, ideas on enhancing the environment and academic programs on campuses trickle up from below. And that is as it should be. But what is the function of the administrator in all this? First, the administrator must accept diversity within the contemporary university and be morally committed to see it flourish. What does it really mean to be committed to diversity? College and university diversity can be defined as the presence and interweaving of all of the complex and varied human and institutional resources that are dedicated to inquiry. These resources especially include minorities whose presence and integration into higher education has been incomplete. The problem is to find effective ways and means to incorporate such groups into the academic community so that they can become valued institutional members, imbued with a sense of ownership. The administrator's commitment inspires participation and interfertilization that sustain the credibility of inquiry and knowledge as cardinal values of the academy.

Second, the administrator must be prepared to provide leadership.

The leader is an advocate in the espousal of the well-defined community values associated with multiculturalism. The administrator represents the values of the community in the moral sense and embodies them in the way that she carries herself. The administrator is seen to be on the side of the best of all our beliefs. She makes statements, offers ideas, helps structure debates, and sets agendas. Others look to the administrator to mix and match and refine their ponderings and musings in a way that helps them reach their goals; they derive their energy to work with this individual from those positive signals.

Leadership advocacy is not just espousal; it must also be demonstrated in the allocation of resources, redistribution of authority, and redesign of structures. It is well understood that words without deeds hardly amount to much. Money must be made available to sustain the task of interweaving members from diverse backgrounds into the university fabric, which must be redesigned to respond to this task. Redistribution of resources must be pursued where an imbalance exists. Leadership advocacy is critically important because of the previous gross negligence in this area. Some of the best efforts in this regard have resulted in the establishment of line offices in academic affairs (staffed with sensitive and experienced personnel) that are responsible for the management of diversity issues in places where the curriculum has been expanded and infused with multicultural courses, and where sensitivity training has become an integral feature of organizational routines.

Third, the administrator must enhance the processes of integrating multiculturalism into the teaching function. The leader must be committed to the independent and essential role of the teaching enterprise in the contemporary academy. It is through teaching that we communicate a set of values and expectations and train students in the general knowledge necessary for a well-rounded education. It must first be established that teaching is of independent and essential importance, notwithstanding research. This priority status means that the administrator accords teaching its proper place in the list of requisites for promotion and tenure. That is to say, teachers must be rewarded for the energy and time that they put into teaching. Moreover, the administrator, having embraced the principles of diversity and multiculturalism, must ensure that the best courses for sustaining the values of diversity constitute a part of every student's general education—much as are math and composition—since these courses encourage the development of critical thinking and communication skills. The challenge of teaching diversity divides into two categories: (1) awareness training, which is usually accomplished extracurricularly and is designed to create sensitivity to previously trampled values and (2) course requirements to provide basic information and intellectual discussion of ethnic and racial cultures (usually regular, general education courses for students).

In sum, in order to respond to the challenges of diversity like the institutions we have described, active leadership and support must come from the administration. Without these attempts to change the system, little progress for multiculturalism can be made on our campuses. The same may be said for financial commitments to programs and activities that strengthen the awareness and information that members of the community have about the integral character of underrepresented groups and their contribution to the academic enterprise of the university.

Conclusion

This chapter has tried to convey the essence of eight approaches to multicultural training in an attempt to expand knowledge and understanding about proven methods. The universities highlighted are not the only ones developing multicultural programs for faculty and teaching assistants, but they do provide examples of current approaches from which other institutions can begin to frame their own programs.

A significant common aspect in the programs described above is institutional commitment. Most of the programs report to a high-level administrative office that provides funding and staff. Administrative support comes in the form of mission statements and commitment to the concept of diversity. These programs also have key administrators involved in the programming. This helps promote departmental interest and involvement because faculty are assured of the administrative legitimacy of the program.

Because faculty are models of behavior for students, creating a change in the classroom environment is crucial. These programs work with faculty to develop programs at the department level with discipline-specific information and case studies. People learn best when they can relate to a problem, practice a solution, and recognize ways to adapt it. The training is designed to enable the participants to deal with tough issues.

One goal common to all the programs is to make sure that staff and volunteers have the knowledge and experience necessary to work with campus community members on such delicate issues as social interaction. In some cases, workshop leaders have brought the expertise with them from their own disciplines. In other cases, programs have added their own training for workshop and seminar leaders. The intention of helping as many people as possible take advantage of the diversity in our institutions will likely lead to highly developed methods of preparing large numbers of facilitators. This is already happening at The Ohio State University, where new facilitators are trained every quarter.

The commitment demonstrated by administrators in the development and implementation stages of these programs must be continued as programs try to reach more individuals and move beyond the "awareness" level to stages of greater depth. Programs are gradually moving beyond racism and gender sensitivity to address other "isms." To improve the effectiveness of programs, evaluation procedures will be able to include more long-term assessment. Dhyana Ziegler, University of Tennessee, Knoxville, made an appropriate summary statement as she discussed the role of the individual in changing the climate of a university. "While it may seem like such a long-term proposition, the [Change Model] project does actually have immediate impact as well—participants meet colleagues who share their visions and ideals, and these small groups can have immediate impact upon committees and university policy. It took, after all is said and done, many, many years to implant distorted ideas about race and race issues in the hearts and minds of people; it will take as much energy, time, and commitment to dig them up and discard them."

DIANE R. VOM SAAL is director of the Program for Excellence in Teaching and assistant professor in Curriculum and Instruction at the University of Missouri, Columbia.

DEBRAH J. JEFFERSON is faculty development specialist in the Program for Excellence in Teaching and assistant professor in the College of Agriculture at the University of Missouri, Columbia.

MINION KC MORRISON is vice provost for Minority Affairs and Faculty Development and professor of political science at the University of Missouri, Columbia.

What we need today are groups of well-informed, caring individuals who band together in the spirit of community to learn from one another, to participate, as citizens in the democratic process
—The Carnegie Report.

The Future Is Now: A Call for Action and List of Resources

Laura L. B. Border, Nancy Van Note Chism

Several common themes run throughout this volume and impose themselves as possible subtitles. *Education from the Bottom Up* would reflect the societal changes that are transforming the traditional university system. *Collaboration in a Traditionally Competitive System* would reflect the idea that collaboration is more effective than competition. A third subtitle might be *Graduation Robes of Many Colors* to reflect the nationwide need to ensure that more students of color graduate.

If the days of rugged individualism in academe are disappearing, it does not mean that no frontiers remain to be claimed and tamed. Institutions of higher education are faced with mammoth challenges and opportunities: the need to respond successfully to societal problems and demands; to meet the needs of an increasingly diverse undergraduate population and an increasingly greying faculty; to keep tabs on the burgeoning technology that surrounds us; and to build a diverse, well-informed, and self-reflective faculty to lead us into the wilds of the twenty-first century.

This volume posits feasible solutions and delineates real challenges for the administrators, faculty, and graduate teachers across the country who face these challenges daily. American culture is and has always been made up of diverse populations. The legacy of the peoples who have settled here represents a rich tapestry of traditions, music, cuisine, vocabulary, hopes, and aspirations. The resulting American culture is both exceptional and exciting. The purpose of this volume is not to encourage the *uni-versity* to become a *di-versity,* but rather to encourage administrators, faculty, and students to attain an even higher level of collaboration and achievement.

NEW DIRECTIONS FOR TEACHING AND LEARNING, no. 49, Spring 1992 ©Jossey-Bass Publishers

What are the implications for administrators, faculty, teaching assistants, faculty developers, and students of bringing multiculturalism to the fore of the postsecondary endeavor? The authors believe that administrators at all institutions—large public universities as well as small, private predominantly white, black, women's, or men's colleges—can determine reward structures that continue to support and maintain an openness to change and experimentation, encourage the re-tooling of their faculties as well as the transformation of departmental curricula, and provide effective support systems for undergraduates.

Faculty and teaching assistants of both genders, all races, and all ethnicities are called on to honestly assess their beliefs, values, and assumptions, as well as their positions on the cultural/linguistic continua described in Chapter Three. Instructors are challenged to examine their individual teaching styles—taking their own inadvertent bias into consideration—to expand the breadth of their knowledge of the diverse cultures represented in their student bodies and to question the depth and breadth of their knowledge of their own disciplines. Professors and teaching assistants also are asked to explore the current research on student interactions and student success as it relates to teacher behaviors and student learning.

Faculty and TA developers have a unique opportunity to work as liaisons and change agents on their own campuses and through national networking organizations. They can assist administrators, department chairs, faculty, and teaching assistants in planning, developing, and implementing multicultural activities that improve teaching and learning across the campus.

Finally, students stand to gain greatly from continued campuswide attention to multicultural issues. Student access can be improved through special recruitment programs. Student retention can be increased through orientation activities that introduce academic culture, curriculum development, and improved methods of instruction. Collaborative learning and active participation in the common search for knowledge can help students to find and articulate their own voices within the framework of the group.

The term *university* implies a bringing together of schools and colleges into one large institution. The word for university in Arabic is *gamaah,* which actually means a *bringing together.* The authors and coeditors of this volume advocate a bringing together of individuals, ideas, resources, research, and aspirations that will help prepare our young people to meet the joys and tribulations of everyday American existence. To that end, in the following pages we include a report on a survey regarding multicultural faculty and TA development programs and a useful list of print and video resources.

Summary of Data from the Survey on the Treatment of Multicultural Issues in Faculty and TA Development Programs

The editors conducted a survey on TA training and faculty development in multicultural, gender, and ethnicity issues during spring semester 1991.

Fifty-three surveys were mailed, with a response rate of 43 percent. Of the twenty-three programs that responded, fifteen provide faculty or TAs or both with exposure to multicultural issues in teaching; the remaining eight universities are planning to follow suit.

Most programs are relatively new. Seven multicultural programs have ties to academic departments, and eleven are provided by a development center. On ten campuses multicultural training is compulsory; it is voluntary on nine. Eleven campuses provide training prior to or during the fall semester; three provide training before or during the spring semester. The majority of programs that responded devote less than five hours to multicultural training, while only one has provided more than twenty hours of training. Almost half of the programs use some type of program evaluation.

Commonalities in the programs' philosophies are evident. The programs surveyed are based on the belief that (1) teachers should model behavior that demonstrates sensitivity to and knowledge of the present and increasing diversity of the student population, (2) teachers should develop interactional skills that allow them to facilitate positive classroom interactions, and (3) teacher attention to diversity improves students' learning and students' overall success in the university arena.

Topics covered by various programs fall into six broad categories: societal issues, policies and reports, learning styles, personal development, teaching strategies, and curriculum development. Societal issues included questions of gender, race, ethnicity, discrimination, sexism, racism, classism, ethnocentrism, ageism, ableism, heterosexism, anti-Semitism, xenophobia, and AIDS. Policies and report issues covered sexual and racial harassment policies, as well as campus demographic reports that take into consideration the makeup of the undergraduate population, including reentry women students. The question of learning styles arose regarding students' involvement in learning, attributing particular learning styles to particular groups, and helping all students learn better. Personal development issues included consciousness raising, self-assessment of bias, and taking more individual responsibility for learning about other groups. Teaching issues involved strategies for teaching in the multicultural classroom, avoiding sexism in the classroom, understanding the various perspectives students bring to courses, using diversity in the classroom as a resource, establishing equity in student participation, and planning for cooperative learning. Another essential topic was the importance of introducing the American concept of multiculturalism and its related issues to international teaching assistants.

Activities common to the various development programs were the typical pre-fall or pre-spring semester orientations and workshops or seminars that take place throughout the academic year. Innovative activities included interactive theater workshops, all-day faculty retreats, case-study sessions, invited speakers followed by discussion, interactive sessions led by multicultural consultants, videotape sessions followed by discussion, sessions on cooperative learning techniques, and performances by one campus's TA development staff.

Personnel involved in training included faculty who specialize in cross-cultural studies, administrators, deans of students, counselors, diversity action committees, minority task force groups, and faculty or TA development staff. Train-the-trainer strategies focused mainly on using senior TAs to train beginning TAs. A list of programs and contact persons follows:

University of Arizona. Multicultural Faculty Development. *Contact:* Connie Gajewski, Coordinator, Affirmative Action Office. TA Training Program. *Contact:* Terri Riffe, Coordinator, University Teaching Center; 1017 N. Mountain, Tuscon, AZ 85721, (602) 621-7788.

Cornell University. Multicultural Faculty Development Program. *Contact:* Jocelyn Hart, Associate Vice President Human Relations, (607) 255-3493. TA Training Program. *Contact:* Rodney Parrott, Coordinator; Multicultural Project, B41 Day Hall, Ithaca, NY 14853-2801, (607) 255-5844.

Edgewood College. Faculty Development Program. *Contact:* Judith Wimmer, Academic Dean; Edgewood College, 855 Woodrow St., Madison, WI 53711, (608) 257-4861.

University of Illinois at Urbana–Champaign. TA and Faculty Development. *Contact:* Dr. Marne Helgesen; Office of Instructional Resources, 307 Eng Hall, 1308 W. Green St., University of Illinois, Urbana, IL 61801, (217) 333-3370.

Indiana University. Faculty Development Program. *Contact:* Linda Annis, Director; Center for Teaching and Learning, Ball State University, Burkhardt Bldg., Rm. 310, Muncie, IN 47306-0205, (317) 285-5422.

Kean College of New Jersey. Faculty Development Program. *Contact:* Madelyn Healy, Director, Center for Professional Development, Kean College of New Jersey, Union, NJ 07083, (201) 527-3113.

Kansas State University. Faculty Development Program. *Contact:* Jane Rowlett, Director, Affirmative Action; Donald Hoyt, Director, Office for Planning and Evaluation Services; Kansas State University, Fairchild Hall, Rm. 215, Manhattan, KS 66506, (913) 532-5712.

University of Maryland. Faculty Development Program. *Contact:* Barbara J. Millis, Assistant Dean; Faculty Development, University of Maryland University College, University Blvd. at Adelphi Rd., College Park, MD 20742, (301) 985-7012.

University of Nebraska–Lincoln. Faculty Development Program. *Contact:* Delivee Wright, Director; Teaching and Learning Center, University of Nebraska-Lincoln, 121 Benton Hall, Lincoln, NE 68588-0623, (402) 472-3079.

University of South Carolina. TA Training Program. *Contact:* Richard Lawhon, Project Coordinator; University of South Carolina, Columbia, SC 29208, (803) 777-4811.

SUNY Stony Brook. Faculty Development Program. *Contact:* Robert Boice, Director; Faculty Instructional Support Office, SUNY-Stony Brook, ECC Building 231, Stony Brook, NY 11794-3700, (516) 632-8356.

Syracuse University. TA Training Program. *Contact:* Leo Lambert, Associate Dean; Graduate School, Syracuse University, Suite 303 Bowne Hall, Syracuse, NY 13244-1200, (315) 443-4492.

University of Tennessee. TA Training Program. *Contact:* W. Lee Humphreys, Director; Learning Research Center, University of Tennessee, 1819 Andy Holt Avenue, Suite #5, Hoskins Library, Knoxville, TN 37996, (615) 974-2459.

University of Texas at Austin. Faculty Development and TA Training Program. *Contact:* Marilla Svinicki, Director; University of Texas at Austin, Main Building 2202, Austin, TX 78712-1111, (512) 471-1488.

University of California at Berkeley. Faculty Development Program. *Contact:* Barbara Gross Davis; Office of Educational Development, University of California-Berkeley, 273 Stephens Hall, Berkeley, CA 94720, (510) 642-6392. TA Training Program. *Contact:* Jacqueline Mintz, Coordinator; GSI Training-Graduate Division, University of California-Berkeley, California Hall, Berkeley, CA 94720, (510) 642-4456.

University of California at Riverside. TA Training Program. *Contact:* Linda B. Nilson, Ph.D., Director; Teaching Assistant Development Program (TADP), University of California-Riverside, 1110 Library South, Riverside, CA 92504, (714) 787-3386.

University of California at San Diego. TA Training Program. *Contact:* John Andrews, Director; University of California-San Diego, 2033 UCSD, La Jolla, CA 92093, (619) 534-6767.

University of Massachusetts at Amherst. Faculty Development Program. *Contact:* Grant Ingle, Director; Office of Human Relations, (413) 545-0851.

TA Training Program. *Contact:* Mary Deane Sorcinelli, Director; Center for Teaching, University of Massachusetts, 160 Whitmore Administration, Amherst, MA 01003, (413) 545-1225.

Print Resources on Multicultural Teaching in Higher Education

Although the body of literature that deals with multicultural education is large, little focuses directly on teaching issues in higher education. In the list that follows, we have tried to cite those sources that treat college settings and directly relate to instructors. Occasionally, a source from another context that is readily transferable is included, especially if the literature base in a particular area is small. A more complete list of readings relevant to the issues treated in each chapter can be found in the reference lists throughout the volume.

Demographic Projections

A variety of sources detail demographic projections indicating the ways in which the student body in higher education will continue to be more diverse. The American Council on Education (Washington, D.C.) issues its Annual Status Report on Minority Participation in Higher Education each year. *Change,* the magazine of the American Association for Higher Education, has published issues containing chapters dealing with demographic characteristics of specific groups: African Americans (volume 19:3, 1987), Hispanic Americans (volume 20:3, 1988), Asian Americans (volume 21:6, 1989), and American Indians (volume 23:2, 1991). Other sources include the following:

Hess, B., Markson, E. W., and Stein, P. J. "Racial and Ethnic Minorities: An Overview." In P. Rothenberg (ed.), *Racism and Sexism: An Integrated Study.* New York: St. Martin's Press, 1988.

   Presents historical and background information on specific cultural groups and the diversity within groups.

Levine, A., and Associates. *Shaping Higher Education's Future: Demographic Realities and Opportunities, 1990–2000.* San Francisco: Jossey-Bass, 1989.

   A treatment of projections with specific information on particular populations and regions. Also includes insights on the interpretation of demographic figures.

Solmon, L., and Wingard, T. L. "The Changing Demographics: Problems and Opportunities." In P. G. Altbach and K. Lomotey (eds.), *The Racial Crisis in American Higher Education.* Albany: State University of New York Press, 1991.

Discusses demographic trends as both a challenge and an opportunity and discusses the ways in which institutions of higher education can work most productively with the issues.

Cultural and Cognitive Characteristics

Descriptions of the worldviews, cultural characteristics, and learning styles associated with particular groups of students are also contained in the issues of *Change* mentioned above, as well as in a variety of other sources. Five articles that discuss the general concept of cognitive style as it relates to culture follow:

Anderson, J. A. "Cognitive Styles and Multicultural Populations." *Journal of Teacher Education,* 1988, *38,* 1–8.
    Differentiates between western and nonwestern worldviews and field-dependent and field-independent learning styles and how they relate to writing styles, classroom learning, and communication.

Banks, J. A. "Ethnicity, Class, Cognitive, and Motivational Styles." *Journal of Negro Education,* 1988, *57,* 452–466.
    Explores the relationship of ethnicity and social class on motivation and learning styles, arguing against the cultural deprivation assumption. Summarizes the implications for teaching.

Griggs, S. A., and Dunn, R. "The Learning Styles of Multicultural Groups." *Journal of Multicultural Counseling and Development,* 1989, *17,* 146–155.
    Reviews cross-cultural research on learning styles and supports a relationship between culture and learning styles. Cautions against stereotypes and stresses individual differences.

Hilliard, A. "Teachers and Cultural Styles in a Pluralistic Society." *NEA Today,* 1989, 65–69.
    Discusses the issue of the possible relationship between culture and learning style and the implications for teaching. Situated in an elementary-secondary context, but applicable to higher education.

Hofstede, G. "Cultural Difference in Teaching and Learning." *International Journal of Intercultural Relations,* 1986, *10,* 301–320.
    Looks at differences based on culturally mixed and unequal status relationships such as teacher-student in the college classroom. Builds a four-dimensional model of cultural differences that can help understand the basis of communication differences.

African American
Shade, B. J. "African American Cognitive Style: A Variable in School Success?" *Review of Educational Research,* 1982, *52,* 219–244.

Reviews pro and con discussions on the existence of a specific African American cognitive style and description of the visual-spatial preferences, concept attainment strategies, categorization and abstraction preferences, and other characteristics noted in the research to date. Centered on children, but applicable to adult learning.

Stikes, C. S. *Black Students in Higher Education.* Carbondale: Southern Illinois University Press, 1984.

Explores through case studies the characteristics of African American students and proposes a model of African-American student development based on these characteristics.

American Indian
Locust, C. "Wounding the Spirit: Discrimination and Traditional American Indian Belief Systems." *Harvard Educational Review,* 1988, *58,* 315–330.

Lists and explains ten statements common to most Indian belief systems and argues that fundamental differences between Indian and non-Indians lead to problems in the classroom and elsewhere.

Thomason, T. C. "Counseling Native Americans." *Journal of Counseling and Development,* 1991, *69,* 321–327.

Identifies four types of Indian households and the expectations and characteristics of students associated with each. From a counseling perspective, but illuminative for teaching and learning issues, particularly with respect to the stress on the diversity of tribe and family background among American Indians.

Tierney, W. G. *Official Encouragement, Institutional Discouragement: Minorities in Academe—The Native American Experience.* Norwood, N.J.: Ablex, 1992. Also see the overview of this study in Tierney, W. G. "Native Voices in Academe: Strategies for Empowerment." *Change,* 1991, *23,* 36–44.

Based on a two-year ethnographic study, this book describes the Native American college experience from the perspectives of students from many tribal, family, and community backgrounds. Explores issues related to class, gender, organizational stratification and contexts, and state and campus environment issues.

Asian American
Bagasao, P. Y. "Student Voices Breaking the Silence: The Asian and Pacific American Experience." *Change,* 1989, *21,* 28–37.

Based on interviews with eleven students on their college experience, this discussion focuses on differences among students and the dangers of stereotyping.

Garner, B. "Southeast Asian Culture and the Classroom Climate." *College Teaching*, 1989, *37*, 127–130.

Describes the backgrounds of Indochinese students, distinguishing among various populations and drawing implications for teaching and learning.

Suzuki, B. H. "Asian Americans as the 'Model Minority.'" *Change*, 1989, *21*, 13–19.

Argues that stereotypes of Asian students create unrealistic expectations and actually result in discrimination in higher education. Uses census data and recent studies to point to differences among various Asian groups.

Women
Baxter Magolda, M. B. "Gender Differences in Epistemological Development." *Journal of College Student Development*, 1990, *31*, 555–561.

Discusses differences found across college men and women in the areas of reasoning, beliefs on the nature of knowledge, and learning preferences.

Belenky, M. F., Clinchy, B. M., Goldberger, N. R., and Tarule, J. M. *Women's Ways of Knowing: The Development of Self, Body, and Mind.* New York: Basic Books, 1986.

Describes the nature of women's knowing and distinguishes it from traditional patterns based on men's thinking.

Hispanic/Latino
Carnegie Foundation for the Advancement of Teaching. "Hispanic Students Continue to Be Distinctive." *Change*, 1988, *20*, 43–47.

Describes college ambitions and vision among Hispanic students.

Olivas, M. A. (ed.). *Latino College Students.* New York: Teachers College Press, 1986.

Contains chapters that describe constraints and success factors associated with college students from several Hispanic groups.

Inclusive Pedagogy
Chism, N., Cano, J., and Pruitt, A. S. "Teaching in a Diverse Environment." In J. D. Nyquist, R. D. Abbott, and D. H. Wulff (eds.), *Teaching Assistant Training in the 1990s.* New Directions for Teaching and Learning, no. 39. San Francisco: Jossey-Bass, 1989.

Looks at the classroom issues and strategies inherent in successful teaching for diversity, focusing on the particular case of the teaching assistant.

Cones, J. H., Noonan, J. F., and Janha, D. *Teaching Minority Students.* New Directions for Teaching and Learning, no. 16. San Francisco: Jossey-Bass, 1983.
    Contains chapters that center specifically on faculty awareness and responsibilities toward diverse students.

Green, M. F. (ed.). *Minorities on Campus: A Handbook for Enhancing Diversity.* Washington, D.C.: American Council on Education, 1988.
    A thorough, overall treatment that contains an extensive chapter devoted to teaching, learning, and curriculum (pp. 131–157).

Hall, R. M., and Sandler, B. R. *The Classroom Climate: A Chilly One for Women?* Washington, D.C.: Association of American Colleges, 1982.
    Addresses the subtle and overt ways in which women face discrimination in the classroom and contains extensive advice for instructors and others on remedying the problems.

Nyquist, J. D., Abbott, R. D., Wulff, D. H., and Sprague, J. (eds.). *Preparing the Professoriate of Tomorrow to Teach.* Dubuque, Iowa: Kendall/Hunt, 1991.
    Contains a section on diversity that addresses teaching and learning issues from the perspective of the teaching associate, but applicable to other faculty as well.

Pemberton, G. *On Teaching the Minority Student: Problems and Strategies.* Brunswick, Maine: Bowdoin College, 1988.
    Discusses the common problems that students of color face and suggests strategies for enhancing the success of both instructors and administrators.

    Although not centered on higher education, two general works that contain important insights that can be transferred into the postsecondary context are *Multiethnic Education: Theory and Practice* by J. Banks (Boston: Allyn & Bacon, 1988) and *Multicultural Education in a Pluralistic Society* by D. M. Gollnick and P. C. Chinn (Columbus, Ohio: Merrill, 1990, 3rd ed.).

Classroom Communication

The particular issues associated with instructor-student communication in the classroom are critical to student success, yet often troublesome when particular cultural backgrounds create different assumptions about communication. Only a few sources discuss these issues with particular respect to the classroom, but several more general treatments contain useful insights that can be transferred.

Kochman, T. *Black and White Styles in Conflict*. Chicago: University of Chicago Press, 1981.
Presents cultural differences and patterns of communication, particularly as they impact classroom communication.

Pearson, J. C., and West, R. "An Initial Investigation of the Effects of Gender on Student Questions in the Classroom." *Communication Education*, 1990, *40*, 22–30.
Based on an observation of fifteen college classrooms, this study describes the impact of teacher and student gender on verbal and nonverbal communication patterns.

Rich, A. L. *Interracial Communication*. New York: Harper & Row, 1974.
Discusses both verbal and nonverbal communication patterns and the ways in which stereotypes and conflicting expectations interfere with communication across cultures.

Sanders, J. A., and Wiseman, J. A. "The Effects of Verbal and Nonverbal Teacher Immediacy on Perceived Cognitive, Affective, and Behavioral Learning in the Multicultural Classroom." *Communication Education*, 1990, *39*, 341–353.
Discusses the verbal and nonverbal dimensions of college classroom teaching with respect to particular student populations.

Tannen, D. *You Just Don't Understand: Women and Men in Conversation*. New York: Ballantine, 1990.
Depicts the ways in which different communication styles between males and females lead to difficulties. A general treatment, although some references are made to classroom interactions.

Wu, J., and Morimoto, K. "On Careful Listening." In J. H. Cones, J. F. Noonan, and D. Janha (eds.), *Teaching Minority Students*. New Directions for Teaching and Learning, no. 16. San Francisco: Jossey-Bass, 1983.
Stresses listening as a means of helping students feel authentic and recognized.

Curriculum Issues

Although the boundaries of this volume did not permit treatment of curriculum issues, two readings that would serve as a good general introduction include:

Botstein, L. "The Undergraduate Curriculum and the Issue of Race: Opportunities and Obligations." In P. G. Altbach and K. Lomotey (eds.), *The Racial Crisis in American Higher Education*. Albany: State University of New York Press, 1991.

Discusses ten practical suggestions for and obstacles to curricular reform and includes a philosophical interpretation of current curriculum debates. Summarizes principles of curriculum design that are related to multicultural inclusion.

Butler, J. E. "Transforming the Curriculum: Teaching About Women of Color." In J. A. Banks and C.A.M. Banks (eds.), *Multicultural Education: Issues and Perspectives*. Boston: Allyn & Bacon, 1989.

Discusses transformation as the process of revealing both unity and differences among human beings. Provides information on cross-ethnic and multiethnic pedagogy, especially with respect to curriculum.

Videotapes on Multicultural Teaching

As campuses develop programs for faculty and teaching assistants on the classroom issues connected with student diversity, many have produced videotapes for use in workshops or presentations. Some are specific to particular campuses and others are more general. There are several videotapes and series, such as those produced by the Bok Center at Harvard University or the Office of Student Affairs at the University of California at Santa Barbara, that concern general campus diversity or student-to-student tolerance. Others, such as the *Valuing Diversity* series or *The Tale of O* have been developed for general purposes or business environments. The videotapes listed below are particularly applicable to the instructor-student issues and the teaching dimensions of multiculturalism in higher education.

√ *Minorities in the College Classroom*
A series of vignettes with instructors in the classroom centers on the subtle and not-so-subtle ways in which stereotyping, biased expectations, and insensitivity can inhibit the academic success of students. (27 minutes. Order from: Department of Human Relations, Michigan State University, 300 Administration Building, East Lansing, MI 48824-1046.)

√ *Making a Difference: Teaching for Black Student Retention*
Focusing exclusively on African American students, this videotape shows students, alumni, faculty, and administrators at The Ohio State University identifying the ways in which classroom teaching constrains the success of African American students, suggesting strategies for change, and listing the reasons why change is important. (24 minutes. Order from: Faculty and TA

Development, Center for Teaching Excellence, Ohio State University, 20 Lord Hall, 124 West 17th Avenue, Columbus, OH 43214.)

Voices in a Campus Community
A general treatment of campus diversity, about half of this videotape treats classroom issues, such as tokenism and curriculum change. Includes the perspectives of different cultures, sexual orientations, and disabilities. (28 minutes. Order from: Equity Steering Committee, School of Education and Human Development, State University of New York at Binghamton, P.O. Box 6000, Binghamton, NY 13902-6000.)

✓ Teaching in a Diverse Classroom
Describes four general strategies recommended by instructors and students for teaching effectively within a diverse classroom: helping all students feel connected to the university, accommodating a variety of learning preferences, creating an environment of respect, and recognizing diversity through curriculum choices. (Approximately 30 minutes. Order from: Center for Instructional Development and Research, 109 Parrington, DC-07, Seattle, WA 98195.)

LAURA L. B. BORDER is director of the Graduate Teacher Program, Graduate School, University of Colorado, Boulder.

NANCY VAN NOTE CHISM is program director for faculty and TA development at the Center for Teaching Excellence, Ohio State University, Columbus.

Index

117

ORDERING INFORMATION

NEW DIRECTIONS FOR TEACHING AND LEARNING is a series of paperback books that presents ideas and techniques for improving college teaching, based both on the practical expertise of seasoned instructors and on the latest research findings of educational and psychological researchers. Books in the series are published quarterly in Fall, Winter, Spring, and Summer and are available for purchase by subscription as well as by single copy.

SUBSCRIPTIONS for 1992 cost $45.00 for individuals (a savings of 20 percent over single-copy prices) and $60.00 for institutions, agencies, and libraries. Please do not send institutional checks for personal subscriptions. Standing orders are accepted.

SINGLE COPIES cost $14.95 when payment accompanies order. (California, New Jersey, New York, and Washington, D.C., residents please include appropriate sales tax.) Billed orders will be charged postage and handling.

DISCOUNTS FOR QUANTITY ORDERS are available. Please write to the address below for information.

ALL ORDERS must include either the name of an individual or an official purchase order number. Please submit your order as follows:
  Subscriptions: specify series and year subscription is to begin
  Single copies: include individual title code (such as TL1)

MAIL ALL ORDERS TO:
  Jossey-Bass Publishers
  350 Sansome Street
  San Francisco, California 94104

FOR SALES OUTSIDE OF THE UNITED STATES CONTACT:
  Maxwell Macmillan International Publishing Group
  866 Third Avenue
  New York, New York 10022

OTHER TITLES AVAILABLE IN THE
NEW DIRECTIONS FOR TEACHING AND LEARNING SERIES
Robert J. Menges, Editor-in-Chief
Marilla D. Svinicki, Associate Editor